Boundaries in the Mind

OTHER BOOKS BY ERNEST HARTMANN

The Biology of Dreaming

Adolescents in a Mental Hospital
(with Betty A. Glassner, Milton Greenblatt, Maida H. Solomon, and Daniel Levinson)

Sleep and Dreaming

The Functions of Sleep

The Sleeping Pill

The Nightmare
(Basic Books)

The Sleep Book

ERNEST HARTMANN

BOUNDARIES IN THE MIND

A New Psychology of Personality

BasicBooks
A Division of HarperCollins*Publishers*

Library of Congress Cataloging-in-Publication Data
Hartmann, Ernest.
Boundaries in the mind : a new psychology of personality / Ernest Hartmann.
p. cm.
Includes bibliographical references and index.
ISBN 0-465-00739-2 (cloth)
ISBN 0-465-00740-6 (paper)
1. Individuality. 2. Personality. 3. Awareness. I. Title.
BF697.H377 1991
155.2—dc20 91-70061 CIP

Copyright © 1991 by BasicBooks,
A Division of HarperCollins Publishers, Inc.

All rights reserved. Printed in the United States of America. No part of this book may be reproduced in any manner whatsoever without written permission except in the case of brief quotations embodied in critical articles and reviews. For information, address BasicBooks, 10 East 53rd Street, New York, NY 10022-5299.

Designed by Ellen Levine

93 94 95 96 CC/CW 9 8 7 6 5 4 3 2 1

CONTENTS

ACKNOWLEDGMENTS

THE IDEAS SUMMARIZED in this book developed slowly over the past years. Many of the ideas as well as the studies done to examine them came from a series of monthly meetings with a wonderful group of people whom I call the "Boundary Investigators" or the "Boundary Bunch." The membership changed from time to time, but I would like to express a sincere debt to all of them (I hope I'm not leaving anyone out): Holiday Adair, Deirdre Barrett, Stephanie Beal, Liz Bernstein, Judith Bevis, William Butler, Hania Dawani, Jonathan Earle, Rachel Elkin, Susan Fagan, Frank Galvin, Mithlesh Garg, Stephanie Hancox, Robert Harrison, Adele Holevas, Irving Hurwitz, Linda Jordan, Robert Kunzendorf, Pamela Newton Renna, Leonard Solomon, Justin Weiss, and Martin Zelin.

I am especially indebted to Bob Harrison, whose unique combination of clinical and teaching experience, statistical expertise, and general feel for things (wisdom) were absolutely essential to our work; to Bob Kunzendorf, a born researcher and a fountain of ideas, who is also more of a clinician than he knows; and to Deirdre Barrett and Frank Galvin, who provided essential constructive criticism over a long period, helped shape the Boundary Questionnaire, and added important new data of their own. Thanks also to Bessel van der Kolk, my long-term collaborator in studies of nightmares. Our many attempts to categorize the personality of the nightmare sufferer eventually led to the concept of thin boundaries, elaborated in this book.

My old friend and colleague Myron Sharaf was helpful in more ways than I can easily summarize. He fell in love with the idea of Boundaries and used it in his clinical work, which I found most gratifying; at the same time he came up with innumerable probing questions and criticisms which we discussed at length and which helped me clarify what I was talking about. This book would be considerably different without him.

I want to thank those who read this manuscript in its various forms, criticized it, and improved it or pushed me to improve it in all sorts of large and small ways. These are my wife Eva Neumann Hartmann, my brother Larry Hartmann, Donald Anderson, Deirdre Barrett, Frank Galvin, Marlene Griffith, Bob Harrison, Anton Kris, Bob Kunzendorf, Myron Sharaf, and Andrea Wilson; and also my editor at Basic Books JoAnn Miller and a very creative copy editor Nina Gunzenhauser. Every one of you had a part in shaping this thing, which by now may sound like a rococo monument rather than a book.

The concept of boundaries in the mind and the various ideas discussed in this book are based on my work with a large number of patients, and with participants in many different research projects. There must be about two thousand people in these categories by now; I want all of them to know that their contributions were absolutely essential to me, whether they took part in long-term therapy, came for research interviews, filled out questionnaires, or took part in laboratory tests.

Last, I would like to dedicate this book to William Francis Butler (1962–1991) a member of our Boundary Investigator group who valiantly continued his studies and his research work on imagery and cancer right up to the time of his own death from cancer early this year.

PART ONE

WHAT ARE BOUNDARIES?

CHAPTER 1

Boundaries: A New Dimension of Personality

OUR WORLD IS FULL of boundaries—boundaries between ourselves and others; boundaries around our family, our group, our country; boundaries between "us" and "them." When we study the geography of the world we live in, we are shown maps and globes on which regions called "nations" are carefully delineated in contrasting colors. Yet these boundaries do not occur in nature as physical entities. All these boundaries really exist only in our minds.

Our temporal world likewise appears to be made up of regions or epochs with boundaries between them. We each have a past, a present, and a future; we move through childhood, adolescence, and adulthood. At any given time we are either awake or asleep. When awake, we have periods of working and periods of playing, periods of physical activity and periods of quiet thinking and feeling. Sometimes the boundaries are sharp, sometimes less distinct; we can be doing several things at once or be in-between states. Again the boundaries are in our minds.

THICK AND THIN BOUNDARIES

When we consider the contents of our minds—thoughts, feelings, memories; ego, id, superego; perceptual processes, semantic processes, memory processes—we are speaking of parts, of regions, functions, or processes that are separate from one another and yet connected with one another. The boundaries between them are not absolute separations: they can be relatively thick or solid on the one hand or relatively thin or permeable on the other.

But boundaries are more than a descriptive concept. I believe that thickness of boundaries represents a neglected dimension of personality, one that can help us understand aspects of our lives that no other measure can explain. As a first approximation of what I mean, there are people who strike us as very solid and well organized; they keep everything in its place. They are well defended. They seem rigid, even armored; we sometimes speak of them as "thick-skinned." Such people, in my view, have very thick boundaries. At the other extreme are people who are especially sensitive, open, or vulnerable. In their minds, things are relatively fluid; they experience thoughts and feelings—often many different feelings—at the same time. Such people have particularly thin boundaries.

Most of us are somewhere in between or have a mixture of boundaries, some thick and some thin. But it is by looking at the extreme cases that we can begin to understand the power of boundaries as an explanatory concept. Consider the following two examples:

"Ah, you have a beautiful purple aura around you; I know I can trust you and talk to you." These were the first words spoken to me by Lavinia, who came to see me not as a psychiatric patient but as a potential subject in a research study. She did trust me and talk to me, and within an hour she had told me more about her life than I usually learn from patients in weeks in my practice. I learned that she has always had powerful, lifelike daydreams and fantasies as well as vivid dreams at night. Sometimes these dreams are so vivid and accompanied by so much feeling that they persist into her waking reality, so that she is not quite sure what state she is in. She is surprisingly in touch with her childhood and has clear, detailed memories from the age of two. She sees herself as always having been an unusually sensitive child. "Everything got to me." In fact there is sometimes too much getting to her: "I can't keep things out." Her family was intact, with no obvious problems, and as far as she knows, she experienced no serious trauma. Yet small traumas made a deep impression on her; for example, the death of a pet produced nightmares and painful feelings that remained with her for months.

Lavinia is an artist and works part-time at another job to support herself. Bright and creative, she becomes involved in many projects but has trouble completing any single piece of work; "I go off on all these interesting tangents; it's hard to get back to what I was working on."

She has had several intense relationships, and in each case she was devastated when the relationship broke up. She trusts people easily, sometimes too easily; she has been assaulted, and on one occasion she was almost raped. She speaks intensely, with emotion, gliding from one subject to another without my having to ask questions. I feel pulled into her life, and my overall sense is of her openness and defenselessness. Lavinia has thin boundaries in almost all the senses I will discuss in this book.

"That's all there is, Doc!" Andrew, a man I have seen for two months in psychotherapy, tries to tell me about his life, but he seems to have little to tell. He never opens a new subject spontaneously. He waits for me to ask him a question and then gives a brief, precise answer. It is not necessarily an unemotional answer; he is quite charming and smiles a lot. But his smile always looks like the same smile. His favorite expressions seem to be "That's it, Doc" and "That's all I can tell you, Doc."

This man is a solid, functioning member of society. He has a decent job; he has a number of friends, though not very close friends. He has had several sexual relationships, but he does not seem to have become intensely involved with the women, nor, for that matter, with anything else in his life. He tends to speak in clichés: things are "not bad," "I can't complain." His mother is "a wonderful woman, Doc, wonderful." He has been told his childhood was "normal," and what he can remember seems "pretty good," but he can remember virtually nothing before the age of seven.

After two months I seem to know less about this man

than I knew about Lavinia in one hour. He comes across as solid and competent but closed, totally defended, full of walls. I feel excluded from his life.

These two people are obviously very different from one another, but in what way exactly? They do not differ greatly in intelligence, or in relative introversion or extroversion, or even in degree of health or illness. Both are functioning members of society, though both clearly have problems. Lavinia could be called "far out" or even "a bit crazy" (though she has never been psychotic), and Andrew could be called "uptight" or "rigid"; I will not go into more technical terms for now. But what I feel differentiates them most clearly is the nature of their boundaries. She is an extreme example of a person with thin boundaries in many senses, and he is a person with thick boundaries.

Obviously people differ in many ways; their minds and their brains are organized differently. Psychology has had some success in describing personality differences—many "personality disorders" and many possible personality dimensions have been delineated—but the picture appears incomplete, and it has been hard to find any links between personality and the organization of the brain. I propose thick and thin boundaries as a broad way of looking at individual differences, a new dimension of personality. As we shall see, the concept relates to, and can be seen as encompassing, a number of more specific personality measures and characteristics such as fantasy-proneness, absorption, defensiveness or defenselessness, openness or self-disclosure, hypnotizability, and amount of dream recall. I shall try to show that it can be useful in understanding human development, relationships, and mental illness and that it may even help us understand the organization of the human brain.

One might say that I am using one term to describe a number of very different characteristics. Does it make any sense to use the word *boundary* to include them all? Do people who have thin boundaries in one sense also have thin boundaries in other senses? Aren't we talking about a number of separate aspects of personality? Do they all relate in some way?

I believe that there is such a relationship and that an overall concept of thin or thick boundaries is a useful one. Rather than attempting to demonstrate these ideas with an abstract discussion or a review of the history of the concept, however, I would like first to describe how I arrived at the notion of thin and thick boundaries. The chapters that follow will then address the above questions and many other issues related to boundaries and personality, including the various types of psychological boundaries and the relationships among them, the measurement of thickness and thinness of boundaries, and the relationships between thickness of boundaries and such variables as age and gender. We will look at how boundaries originate and develop and consider the crucial question of whether boundaries can change over a person's lifetime. We will consider how thickness or thinness of boundaries relates to sleep and dreaming as well as to physical and mental illness. This issue will lead to a discussion of the potential usefulness of the concept of boundaries, with a close examination of the relationship between boundaries and creativity and madness. Are certain kinds of boundaries adaptive or maladaptive?

Can knowledge of a person's boundary structure help us to make a difference practically or clinically? In addition to discussing its practical and theoretical usefulness, I will suggest that the concept of boundaries may also represent an aspect of the biology of the brain.

FROM NIGHTMARES TO BOUNDARIES

My interest in boundaries began some years ago, when I was intensively studying dreams and nightmares. As a psychoanalyst and therapist, I have always listened carefully to my patients' dreams, which can indeed serve as the "royal road to the unconscious" (Freud 1900). As a researcher in sleep and sleep disorders, I have done many studies relating dreams with medical and psychological conditions. And as a scientist trying to understand the human mind, I have been constantly intrigued by the enigma of waking and dreaming consciousness: we possess one mind, one brain, yet it is capable of two such different forms of functioning, producing two very different forms of consciousness. Understanding the differences and relationships between waking and dreaming at each psychological and biological level should help us understand our minds. And finally, I have always been fascinated by my own dreams.

The nightmare is perhaps the most intense form of dream—vivid, gripping, and all too real. Anything we can learn about this terrifying form of dreaming might tell us about other dreams as well. And anyone who has had nightmares is intrigued by them, not only because they are so frightening but perhaps also because they are so separate, so "out there," so much something that is happening to us and yet coming from within us.

I became intrigued by the question of who has nightmares. A majority of adults claim they have either no nightmares or at most two or three a year (Hartmann 1984). College students report somewhat more than this (Belicki 1987; Wood and Bootzin 1990). Yet I have met a number of successful, apparently normal adults who have nightmares almost every night. Four of these people told me they considered their nightmares so much a part of their lives that they assumed everyone had nightmares all the time; they were rather surprised to learn that their situation was unusual.

To find out who has nightmares, my colleagues and I chose to study people who responded to newspaper ads asking for volunteers who were willing to discuss their nightmares and their lives, to take psychological tests, and in some cases to be studied in the sleep laboratory (Hartmann 1984; Hartmann et al. 1981; Hartmann, Russ, et al. 1987).

As a psychiatrist and a sleep disorder specialist I have seen many patients with nightmares and with other sleep-related conditions. I decided, however, that this would not make the best population to answer our basic question, since they were a special group who were seeking help, and obviously saw their nightmares as a problem requiring help. Furthermore, the demands of research and of psychotherapy do not coincide. It is always difficult and at times may be unethical to attempt to do objective research with someone you are simultaneously trying to help in psychotherapy. We therefore advertised for people who had frequent nightmares but no other sleep-related conditions.

We recruited fifty subjects, twenty to fifty years old, with lifelong histories of nightmares, who did not have night terrors or other sleep disorders. Two separate studies were conducted. The first study group consisted of thirty-eight persons, two-thirds women and one-third men, all of whom reported frequent nightmares. In the second study, twelve subjects with frequent nightmares were compared with two control groups—one consisting of twelve people who reported no nightmares but very vivid dreams, the other made up of twelve people who had neither nightmares nor vivid dreams. In the second study, each group was evenly split between men and women.

What characterized the fifty people with nightmares and differentiated them from the other groups? First of all, it was not simply psychopathology. Psychiatrists and psychologists who see people with nightmares in the course of various mental illnesses often have the impression that people with nightmares must be mentally ill in some way. To examine this issue, we attempted to determine, on the basis of interviews, whether any of the subjects in the studies fit the criteria for any sort of mental illness or disorder, as defined in DSM-III, the *Diagnostic and Statistical Manual of Mental Disorders* (1980), compiled by the American Psychiatric Association. It was possible to make such a diagnosis in only one-third of those with nightmares. Even in these subjects, the diagnoses were rarely what *DSM-III* classifies as clinical disorders—that is, mental illness—but almost always personality disorders, most frequently "schizotypal," "schizoid," or "borderline" personality disorder. In four cases an actual mental illness—schizophrenia—could be diagnosed. In the two control groups, no one could be given a definite psychiatric diagnosis, although some came close.

These findings do indicate some tendency to a certain kind of pathology, sometimes called "schizophrenia spectrum" pathology, in the nightmare sufferers. Interestingly, none of them had other serious mental illness such as manic-depressive illness, other depressions, or the various anxiety disorders. And perhaps most important, two-thirds of the people with frequent nightmares could be given no diagnosis whatever. In other words, they had no diagnosable mental illness or condition, not even a personality disorder.

When we turned our attention away from pathology, we were struck by a number of unusual characteristics of these people with frequent nightmares—characteristics not found in the control groups, who had also answered newspaper advertisements. For one thing, they had somewhat atypical life styles. None of them were average blue-collar or white-collar workers. Many had jobs relating to the arts or crafts; several were musicians, and some were teachers or therapists, often art or music teachers or art therapists. Thus their jobs were in artistic or creative fields, and indeed most of them described themselves as having been artistic or creative in some way even in childhood. In contrast the control groups had a very average mix of occupations.

Almost all the nightmare sufferers described themselves as being unusually sensitive. Some meant sensitive in a perceptual way—easily bothered by bright lights or loud sounds. Most meant easily hurt emotionally, some meant unusually empathic, and some meant all of the above, and more.

These subjects were also unusually open. My colleagues and I have interviewed close to a thousand patients and subjects in various research studies, so we have a fairly good idea of what someone will tell you in an initial interview. Most research subjects are cooperative, willing to answer questions in the interests of science, but at the same time they are somewhat guarded; they usually do not reveal more than is asked for, and they are not anxious to discuss things such as painful family secrets. Research subjects tend to be less open than patients entering psychotherapy. But the nightmare subjects were different. They were surprisingly unguarded; they opened up immediately and shared all kinds of painful problems, including sexual concerns, criminal matters, and skeletons in the family closet. We were amazed at how much such difficult and emotional material emerged, even in the first thirty to sixty minutes.

The nightmare subjects also appeared very trusting, often overly trusting. They revealed a tendency to become involved quickly in relationships that sometimes proved very painful. Sometimes they became involved with inappropriate partners; a few had been physically abused by their partners. They were willing to walk alone, or at night, in neighborhoods most people shunned or entered only with great caution. Again there were sometimes serious consequences; two of the women had been the victims of assaults or attempted rapes.

Another aspect of being unguarded was that these subjects seemed undefended, in a number of psychological senses. They did not repress dangerous material, keeping it out of consciousness; they did not isolate thought from feeling, as many people do, keeping things manageable by not letting themselves get too emotionally involved; they did not intellectualize. In general they did not seem to have readily available to them the various defense mechanisms with which most of us shield ourselves psychologically.

Most members of the nightmare group could be called vulnerable in one way or another. Perhaps because of their openness and trustfulness, they were often taken advantage of. Aside from actual traumatic events, these people with nightmares appeared to be hurt easily. The ordinary tragedies of life—rejections, losses, disagreements with others close to them—were more painful to them than to most people.

During the interviews, careful histories were taken concerning childhood and adolescence. One of our interests was to determine whether the qualities just mentioned—the openness, trusting nature, vulnerability, artistic tendencies, and sensitivity—had always been there, or whether they had appeared at a later time in childhood or adolescence, perhaps after a traumatic event. Of course we were also interested in whether the nightmares themselves had been present since early childhood or had begun after a particular event.

The data we obtained definitely supported the first set of conjectures. These were not people with clear histories of childhood abuse, neglect, and trauma. Many of them became interested in finding out whether a specific event had initiated their nightmares and asked their parents whether anything very traumatic or unusual had occurred early in their lives, which they might have forgotten. Somewhat to our surprise, nothing much emerged. These subjects did not appear to have suffered severe trauma to any greater degree than those in the control groups or others we have interviewed. Of course, information about childhood trauma is not easy to obtain. We all forget or repress a great deal about our own childhoods, and in some cases parents may have reason to hide traumatic events, especially traumas involving sexual or physical abuse by the parents themselves or by close relatives. Yet such situations—events both denied by the parents, and repressed by the children—would hardly be likely to occur in a large proportion of the fifty families. Thus I consider it unlikely, though not completely impossible, that some early, forgotten traumatic event was responsible for initiating the nightmares and the personality characteristics described.

Rather, the impression we obtained was that these people had been open, sensitive, vulnerable, and artistic right from early childhood. They did remember difficult periods and even traumatic periods in their lives, but these were the ordinary traumas of childhood. For example, they would discuss in great detail how devastated they had been by the birth of a younger sibling or by being left by their parents with other relatives for a few days or weeks. It seems that they were already unusually sensitive and reacted unusually strongly to the usual traumas and troubles of childhood.

Adolescence, too, was a difficult time for most of our nightmare sufferers. Again it was not severe external trauma, but rather a series of stormy relationships and a tendency to be easily hurt that characterized the group.

In a general way, the nightmare sufferers were flexible or fluid in their identities and social relationships. They found it easy to imagine themselves as members of the opposite sex, and they often had dreams in which they were members of the other sex. Many were bisexual in their fantasies, and a few in their behavior. When we tried to describe these people globally, some of the words mentioned above kept coming up: "unguarded," "undefended," "fluid," "artistic," "vulnerable," "open." The term that seemed best to encompass all this was that they had "thin boundaries" in many different senses. Everything in their minds seemed to flow together. They did not separate things out, nor did they have barriers or walls to separate themselves from the world.

In following up this line of thought, we were able to show that they in fact saw thin boundaries in the well-known Rorschach projective test, in which one is asked to describe whatever one sees in ten different inkblots. In our second study, the twelve nightmare subjects, twelve vivid dreamers, and twelve non-dreamers all took Rorschach tests, which were scored on a blind basis. There were no differences between the groups on any of the standard scales involving number of responses, form, and movement (Exner 1986). In order to examine boundaries, however, we had developed a detailed scoring system based on the work of Blatt and Ritzler (1974) and of Fisher and Cleveland (1968). We scored for "thin boundaries" or "boundary deficit", by totaling all responses that involved amorphousness ("this is like an amoeba," "a cloud"), loss of shape ("a face that's melting"), merging, and penetration ("a frog being cut apart") or loss of distance ("it's looking at me"). On this scale the nightmare sufferers scored significantly higher than the other groups. (Sivan 1983; Hartmann 1984; Hartmann, Sivan et al., 1984).

In other words these people with frequent nightmares seemed to be characterized by thin or permeable boundaries, by fluidity, by merging, in a number of different psychological senses. And there were hints that this characteristic was true in at least some biological sense as well, for instance with regard to the states of waking and sleep. Some people maintain absolutely clear (thick) boundaries between sleep and waking: they are asleep, and then, in an instant, they are awake, and that's it; there is no blurring, no in-between state. The nightmare sufferers were at the other extreme: they frequently spent time half-asleep or half-awake, in states of drowsiness or in reverie. They described periods of half an hour or longer in the morning when they were not sure whether they were awake or asleep, especially when they had had a vivid dream.

Our overall conclusion was that the people with nightmares could be described as having thin boundaries in all these senses. We became intrigued by the concept of boundaries, since it appeared to represent at the very least a personality dimension that had been neglected. We could easily see that some people, such as those described above, had thin boundaries overall; that some people were "thick" through and through; and that most of us are probably somewhere in between or have a mixture of thin and thick boundaries. It appeared possible that boundary structure might be related to many aspects of life—career choice, relationships with others, health and illness. And knowledge of boundary structure could help us achieve a more complete picture of how our minds are organized.

We were then faced with the question of how to measure boundaries in a wider population. The nightmare studies had depended on painstaking interviews and Rorschach tests administered by skilled interpreters; these would not be practicable methods of gathering information on large numbers of subjects. On the basis of the earlier work and other interview studies, however, I felt that much could be learned about a person's boundaries through the use of a self-administered questionnaire. Admittedly, a questionnaire loses the richness of a clinical interview; one cannot make use of nonverbal cues, emotional tones, and so on. And a questionnaire of course is limited to answers given by a subject on a conscious level: it cannot tap projected unconscious material, as a Rorschach presumably can. A questionnaire therefore cannot be sensitive to types of boundaries of which the subject is completely unaware. On the plus side, however, a questionnaire has the great advantage that it can be filled out by the subject and scored rapidly by a computer or a relatively unskilled technician. The scoring is very reliable; there is almost no room for disagreement.

We therefore developed the Boundary Questionnaire, using data originally derived from the nightmare groups and others. It was designed to include questions about as many different aspects of boundaries and types of boundaries as possible. There are items about interpersonal boundaries ("I expect other people to keep a certain distance") and many kinds of internal boundaries ("Sometimes I don't know whether I'm thinking or feeling," "I have had the experience of not knowing whether I was imagining something or it was actually happening"). The items draw on preferences ("I like houses where rooms have definite walls and each room has a definite function"), habits ("When I am working on a project I make a careful detailed outline and then follow it closely"), and opinions ("I believe many of the world's problems could be solved if only people trusted each other more"). Subjects are asked not only to report actual experiences in the present ("When I read something, I get so involved that it can be difficult to get back to reality") and the past ("I have had déjà vu experiences") but also to project themselves into imagined situations ("I think I would enjoy being the captain of a ship"). Each item is rated by the subject on a scale of 0 ("Not at all true of me") to 4 ("Definitely true of me"). The questionnaire is reproduced and discussed in detail in chapter 4.

To date the questionnaire has been taken by about two thousand people. What we have learned about the thickness and thinness of boundaries in our sample will be described in part II. Before proceeding to the results of these studies, however, let us first look more closely at the nature and variety of boundaries, which will be the subject of chapter 2, and at the relationship of the concept of boundaries to its precursors in earlier literature, to be described in chapter 3.

CHAPTER 2

A New Mental Map: Types of Boundaries

THE CONCEPT of thin or thick boundaries in the mind is clearly a very broad one. It includes many personality characteristics or traits that one would not necessarily consider to be related. They were all found together in the people with nightmares, however, as well as in some other groups to be discussed in later chapters. There seems a good possibility, therefore, that the different sorts of boundaries may have something in common and that examining them together may provide an interesting and useful perspective.

To explain just what I mean by boundaries in the mind, I will discuss briefly a number of different types of boundaries. I realize that not all the types of boundaries listed nor all the examples will be familiar to all readers; we all conceptualize the content and structure of our minds in somewhat different ways. Nonetheless, no matter how we visualize our minds and our relationship to the world, the concept of boundaries can be meaningful. Whatever two entities in our minds or our worlds we are talking about, they can be conceptualized as relatively separate (having a thick boundary between them) or in closer communication (with a thinner boundary between them). Similarly, most of us feel or think of some kind of boundary around ourselves, between us and the world; again this can be a firm or solid separation (thick), like a wall or coat of armor, or less firm and easily penetrable (thin).

Thus the following discussion of types of boundaries uses terms derived not only from classical psychology and from psychoanalysis but from common sense and experience. The illustrative quotations and descriptions are all taken directly from patients, students, or research subjects who scored either very thick or very thin on the Boundary Questionnaire. A summary of the types of boundaries appears in table 1.

PERCEPTUAL BOUNDARIES

Sensation and Sensory Input

Boundaries exist even at the simple level of input to our various senses. The inputs may be completely separate and distinct or they may be joined, associated with other input in some way. Looking at a picture, a person with thick boundaries says, "I see a brown house on a green meadow; that's it." Someone with very thin boundaries might say, "The light in this picture is so

Table 1 Types of Boundaries

- Perceptual boundaries
  - Between sensory inputs
  - Sensory focus or "bandwidth"
  - Around perceptual entities
- Boundaries related to thoughts and feelings
  - Between two thoughts or two feelings
  - Between thought and feeling
  - Around thoughts and feelings (free association)
- Boundaries related to states of awareness or states of consciousness
- Sleep-dream-wake boundaries
  - Between sleep and waking
  - Between dreaming and waking
  - In and around the dream
  - Daydreaming
- Boundaries related to play
- Boundaries related to memory
  - Early memories
  - Recent memories and memory organization
  - Personal past
  - Future plans
- Boundaries around oneself (body boundaries)
  - Barriers against stimuli
  - The skin as a boundary
  - Posture and musculature as boundaries
  - Personal space
- Interpersonal boundaries
- Boundaries between conscious and unconscious and between id, ego, and superego
- Defense mechanisms as boundaries
- Boundaries related to identity
  - Sexual identity
  - Age identity: Between adult and child
  - Constancy of identity
- Group boundaries
- Boundaries in organizing one's life

Table 1 (*Continued*)

Boundaries in environmental preferences
Boundaries in opinions and judgments
Boundaries in decision making and action

thick I can almost taste it" or "That white paint on the shutters is shrill—I can hear a high-pitched note in it." The latter experiences are referred to as *synesthesia,* the coming together of perceptions from different sense modalities, or more technically, the occurrence of imagery in one sense modality in response to sensations in another. Sensitivity to any sensory input is also a type of boundary, referring to how much one "lets in." This is discussed in detail on page 33.

Sensory Focus or "Bandwidth"

Some people appear to focus sharply and cleanly on one thing in the environment, examine it, and go on to the next thing; this is a type of thick boundary. Those with thin boundaries have a broader and perhaps fuzzier focus. They take in a number of things at once; they may be said to be tuned to a broad band of input. Visually one can think of a sharp, intensely focused spotlight beam versus a more diffuse one. One person whose scores indicate extremely thin boundaries says, "There's too much coming in at once; I can never focus on just one thing at a time." This sort of experience has sometimes been thought of as an aspect of schizophrenia, and it certainly occurs in patients during the onset of a psychotic episode (Bowers 1974), but I have also heard it from people who appear to have thin boundaries in many senses yet who have no evidence of mental illness.

Boundaries Around Perceptual Entities

Does one see, hear, smell one thing as a complete entity, or is it always merged or connected to other things? A thick boundary here might be expressed as "That's a white clapboard house, two stories high" versus "That's an interesting-looking white house; I wonder if it's in southern Vermont. It reminds me of the house that . . . ," which would represent a thin boundary. In other words the person with thin boundaries does not stop with the percept of the house but immediately connects it to other percepts, feelings, memories, and so on. A thin boundary here involves an immediate tendency to free associate.

BOUNDARIES RELATED TO THOUGHTS AND FEELINGS

Like sensations, thoughts can be kept individual and separate. People with thick boundaries stick to one thought, think it through to completion, and then stop or go on to something else. At the thin extreme, each thought branches out, connects to other thoughts, and brings other things to mind. The process is rich, but may sometimes be confused; often there is no sense of completion.

One bright, artistic woman described looking something up in an encyclopedia: "I start to read the entry and think about it, but it leads me to other things I need to look up first. And then my eye gets caught by nearby entries that seem related, and I get into those. There's so much fascinating stuff, it may be hours before I get back to the question I started with."

Boundaries between two feelings are more difficult to identify, but here, too, some people seem to experience a single straightforward, circumscribed feeling and stop there—"He hit me, so I got really angry," "I won the race and it felt great!"—while others, those with thin boundaries, glide from one feeling into another or have mixtures of feelings difficult to put into single words. One may have to make up new words or word-combinations to describe the feelings. One may find words in other languages; for instance, there is a useful Anglo-Saxon word *teen,* meaning sorrow-anger.

Boundaries between thought and feeling can also be thick or thin. For people with thick boundaries, thought is one thing, feeling another. If you have a problem, you think your way through it, using pure logical thought; feeling is kept out: "Feelings just get in the way of making the right decision." Feelings exist, of course, but they are kept in their place. After a fine meal you feel good; when you have a cold, you feel lousy; sex feels great. But you don't feel while you're thinking. Thick boundaries can also involve a defensive avoidance of feeling, which will be discussed under defenses.

People with thin boundaries are likely to combine thought and feeling: "All important thought involves feeling, too;" "I can't imagine making a decision without really feeling my way into it." They may well come to conclusions and make decisions without being sure whether they were deciding on the basis of thought or of feeling or both. Yeats was expressing a clear preference for this thin-boundary style when he wrote:

God guard me from those thoughts men think
In the mind alone;
He that sings a lasting song
Thinks in a marrow-bone.
(W. B. Yeats, "A Prayer for Old Age")

Related to the boundaries between thoughts, between feelings, or between thoughts and feelings is the ability or tendency to associate. A person with thick boundaries prefers a straightforward linear thinking and problem solving, and finds it very difficult to free-associate, as in psychotherapy, where the therapist may instruct the patient, "Just tell me what comes to mind." The thick-boundary person cannot do this easily; nothing comes to mind until a specific topic is suggested. Such a person is likely to say, "Just ask me some questions, and I'll be glad to answer them." When I think of several people with very thick boundaries whom I have seen in therapy, several phrases they use come to mind: "Well, that's it," "That's how it is," "There's nothing more to say." Attempts at free-associating quickly come to an end.

For the thin-boundary person, one thought leads right to another, one image to another, often with feeling attached. It is easy to free-associate, sometimes too easy. Such a person does it all the time, outside of therapy as well as inside. The problem, often, is being able to stop.

BOUNDARIES RELATED TO STATES OF AWARENESS OR CONSCIOUSNESS

For thick-boundary people, the states of awareness are totally separate and distinct. When not actually asleep, they are mostly in an ordinary waking, thinking state. Once in a while they may dream or have a daydream while lying on a couch. For thin-boundary people, there are many in-between states. They spend considerable time in reverie, in daydreaming, or in indefinite states, and they move easily from one state to another.

One man with thick boundaries says, "I don't remember my dreams; I don't have daydreams; I don't really have fantasies much. Well, I guess I do; I sometimes think what it would be like to be a millionaire. But that seems silly unless I can make plans about actually making the money." Thick boundaries in this sense involve a certainty, a comfortable sureness that one is here, now, fully awake; other states are occasional, odd, or quirky.

Thin boundaries involve easy merging into fantasy or vivid memory, at times not being quite clear what state one is in. People with thin boundaries in this sense get lost in fantasy, have déjà-vu or jamais-vu experiences. One of the questions on the Boundary Questionnaire that best predicts overall thin boundaries is "I have had the experience of someone calling me or speaking my name and not being sure whether it was really happening or I was imagining it."

SLEEP-DREAM-WAKE BOUNDARIES

For a person with thick boundaries, the transition from sleep to waking is rapid and clear-cut. "I just snap awake in the morning. It's like something clicks and I'm wide-awake." By contrast, someone with very thin boundaries insists, "It often takes me half an hour or an hour to make sure I'm really awake in the morning, especially when I've just had a vivid dream."

The person with thick boundaries tends to remember few dreams. Such a person, waking from a dream, is immediately totally awake, with no connections to the dream, no in-between states. For the thin-boundary person, the dream may continue into waking; in particular, the feeling of the dream seems to last. There may be in-between states of not being sure whether one is dreaming or awake! "When I've had a vivid emotional dream it stays with me for hours, sometimes all day; I can't shake it off. Sometimes it gets in the way: sometimes how I feel with people I meet that day has more to do with the feeling from my dream than with what the people actually say or do."

If one has thick boundaries, the dream is set off from the rest of one's life. If one remembers dreams at all, they are like movies that one watches, or sometimes movies that one acts in. One then wakes up. Period.

For someone with very thin boundaries, things are not so simple. The thin-boundary person remembers many dreams; some are stories, while others are intense fragments or series of images. The dreamer may be someone else in the dream: people with very thin boundaries say that in their dreams they are frequently a member of the opposite sex or even an animal. One woman tells me she has frequent dreams of being a large white bird. The person with thin boundaries may have false awakenings or dreams within dreams: "I have these dreams where something kind of scary is happening, and I wake up. I'm in bed, I get up and start doing my regular things, but then someone comes into the room who lives far away, or someone who's dead, like my father. Then I guess I must still be dreaming, and finally I wake up again, and I'm now really awake in my real bed." People with thin boundaries are also more likely to have lucid dreams, in which they become aware, while still in the dream, that they are dreaming (Galvin 1990); here dreaming consciousness and waking consciousness are present simultaneously.

Boundaries around daydreaming may well be the same thing as, or closely related to, boundaries between states of awareness. People with thick boundaries don't spend much time daydreaming. When they do daydream, they tend to have a well-delineated, sometimes even purposeful daydream that often sounds like a problem-solving session: "I can see myself doing such and such" or "Let's see if I can figure out this problem . . ." Thin-boundary people spend a lot of time in daydreams, which are usually vivid, lifelike, and disorganized. It is not always clear where the daydream stops and ordinary consciousness begins. And the daydreams do not always stay in control; Some people with thin boundaries describe having "daymares," when the day-dream takes on a life of its own, out of their control, and then develops into something frightening, like a nightmare.

BOUNDARIES RELATED TO PLAY

Closely related to daydreams and fantasies is the whole realm of play, important to all children and in some sense to all adults as well. Remembering their play as children, people with thin boundaries speak of having become deeply involved in play, believing in it, getting lost in it. For them play was very real and at times even erupted into everyday life, so that they were not quite sure what was play and what was real. And what they recall is usually unstructured fantasy-play, "free play," or make-believe. People with thick boundaries recall being less involved in free-floating play. For them play usually had a more structured or organized form, and was well demarcated from the rest of life. When they think of play, they think of activities such as team sports or board games.

BOUNDARIES RELATED TO MEMORY

Most of us remember little of the first years of our lives. Freud used the term *primal repression* to refer to our pushing out of consciousness memories from before the age of five or six—memories thought to be connected with the dangerous wishes and feelings of the Oedipus complex. Others explain the same phenomenon by the fact that our memory storage and retrieval mechanisms are not yet in their mature forms, so that memories laid down at that time are not easily retrievable by our different, more mature adult memory systems.

In any case most people have a boundary separating their early years, when almost nothing is remembered, from later years, when memories are relatively well recalled and form a connected whole. A thick boundary in this sense involves a relatively late and solid dividing line, or massive primal repression. Two different patients with very thick boundaries insisted to me, "I can't remember anything that happened to me before the age of eight." One added, "My real, definite memories don't begin until age ten." One woman with very thin boundaries recalled a great deal from the age of two to two and a half; she was herself surprised at being able to recall so much from those years, but she checked her memories with her parents, who confirmed them in detail. Another woman with thin boundaries had over many years vivid dreams and memories of a particular house. At adolescence she finally discussed these with her mother, who was amazed: the memories definitely referred to the house they had lived in when the daughter was an infant; when the child was fourteen months old, they had moved to another city and she had never seen the house again.

With regard to recent memories, the differences are not in the ability to recall; almost everyone can recall recent events quite well. Boundaries here involve how the memories are organized and used. A thick boundary implies that memories are kept in tight compartments and used only when a specific memory compartment is useful to a problem in the present. People with very thick boundaries deal with problems in the present and plan for the future; they call up specific memories when needed and then put them back neatly in their places, as though they were pulling out a folder and putting it back in the filing cabinet. People with thin boundaries in this sense have their memories always with them to some extent. They live in the past as well as the present. It is as though they had folders not neatly filed away but lying around on a messy desk, always being glanced at and perhaps used in their current life. Moreover, the memories are often vivid and real, so that memories, fantasies, and current reality can be difficult to separate.

Another aspect of boundaries related to memory involves one's relationship to one's personal past. The thick view is basically to put the past behind one and go on to face today's challenges. People with thin boundaries here are very involved in their personal past; the past is always there, in and out of awareness.

Boundaries involving memory are also closely related to boundaries involving future plans. A thick boundary here means having precise, well-laid plans for the future, based on the past, of course, but kept separate: "I can lay out pretty well what I expect to be doing each year for the next few years." Thin boundaries mean living in a web of past, present, and future without clear demarcations. Everything is interconnected; the future appears to depend on so many factors that it is almost impossible to know what one will be doing a few years from now.

BOUNDARIES AROUND ONESELF, BODY BOUNDARIES

Barriers Against Stimuli

Several body boundaries form barriers between the self and the outside world. First, we all have some kind of psychophysiological barrier against outside stimuli—bright lights, loud sounds, and the like. Thin boundaries in this sense means having relatively little protection, being very sensitive to and often bothered by stimuli. One woman told me, "My boyfriend and I are very close; we're thinking of getting married. But I can never let him spend the whole night in my bed or even in a bed right next to mine. I hear him moving, I feel the sheets move, I hear the bed shift, and it keeps me awake all night. And it's not just my boyfriend; anyone else is worse. I've never been able to sleep with anyone else in the room."

Bergman and Escalona (1949) provide beautiful clinical descriptions of children who had unusually severe sensitivities of this kind at a very early age:

> Stella . . . was apparently sensitive to light from an early age on. She used to jerk her head away when sunlight hit her. Her eyes used to squint in broad daylight. Riding in the car at night, she used to blink and duck her head when exposed to lights. . . . Stella used to cry when she heard a loud voice or a clap of her hands. She . . . never banged on the piano but rather played it very softly. . . . Stella used to be very sensitive to cold air; it made her "screw up" her face. Hot weather . . . seemed also to cause her discomfort. (p. 337)

In fact, the authors refer to this condition as an "unusually thin protective barrier."

The Skin as a Boundary

For some people the boundary between inside the body and outside is absolute and constant. The body boundary does not change; things are quite clearly either inside or outside. This is a type of thick boundary. Others have a less solid or definite sense of their skin as a body boundary; when they are very relaxed—taking a warm bath, for instance, or dozing off—their bodies may seem to enlarge and merge with the surroundings. They may have a sense of merging with another person physically when kissing or making love, and of merging in a less physical way when feeling in love or feeling very close to someone else. Some people, at times of stress and illness, have a very disturbing sense of loss of body boundary; they may feel that parts of their bodies are changing shape and size or that their insides are coming out of their bodies.

Posture and Musculature as Boundaries

Body boundaries are also reflected in posture and musculature. Although the muscles are not literally at the boundary of the body, as the skin is, the body's muscles function to express what is going on in the mind and brain, and in some people the muscles express a great deal about their boundaries. People with very thick boundaries characteristically hold their bodies—especially their chests, shoulders, and arms—in a solid, tight fashion that suggests "nolle mi tangere" (don't touch me; keep away!). Sometimes this looks like a defensive posture, a fortress posture. It is often quite unconscious: the person is seldom aware of it, though others notice and may think of that person as "rigid" or "tight." Those with very thin boundaries give the opposite impression: soft, fluid, flexible, sometimes with a lack of solidity, as though the body might come apart. Sometimes their bodies seem to be inviting contact or reaching out to touch one.

Personal Space

Another related type of boundary involves the space around the body. A type of thick boundary is the requirement for a clear space—perhaps several feet in each direction—that one does not want others to enter. Someone with thin boundaries in this sense is much more willing to let others in. Cultural patterns and socioeconomic factors influence this measure greatly, but within a given cultural or social group one still finds great differences among individuals, and these appear to be related to a type of boundary. One of my patients with very thick boundaries in many senses describes liking to keep just two feet of space between himself and anyone he is talking with. He is greatly annoyed by people who come closer and invade his space. He hates being in a tightly packed crowd, as in an elevator. Another loves skiing but hates ski lifts, especially chair lifts, because they force him to sit just a few inches from someone else.

I have made an observation relevant to this boundary, based on watching numerous couples and friends walking together—people whom I know to have either quite thick or quite thin boundaries. Two people with thick boundaries walk in neat parallel lines, remaining two to three feet apart. When two people with thin boundaries walk together, the distance between them varies; the lines converge and diverge, bringing them sometimes far apart and sometimes very close together.

INTERPERSONAL BOUNDARIES

The last examples not only dealt with body boundaries and space around onself but touched on the larger and more complex concept of interpersonal boundaries. A great part of human relationships in general, and certainly a major part of psychotherapy, deals with one aspect or another of interpersonal boundaries—one's closeness to or distance from others.

Thick boundaries in this sense can mean having a very solid, separate sense of self: "In any relationship I always remain myself; I don't change." They can mean always keeping a certain emotional distance between oneself and others. Having thick boundaries certainly implies not becoming overinvolved and can also imply being careful, not becoming involved with anyone rapidly.

Thin interpersonal boundaries refer to the opposite tendencies: becoming involved rapidly and deeply and at times losing one's sense of self in a relationship. Having thin boundaries here sounds like falling in love in the ideal romantic sense of merging with the beloved person. The realities of love in someone with thin boundaries, however, can be less than ideal. One woman with very thin boundaries whom I saw in psychotherapy was deeply involved in a relationship in which her boyfriend periodically took drugs, became suspicious of her, flew into a rage, and beat her up. When I pointed out these realities to her and asked her at least to consider taking action to change things, she would say, "Yes, I know all that, but I'm in love with him. It's like he's part of me now. There's no way I can give him up." In her case change was especially difficult because she was repeating a pattern from the previous generation: her father constantly pushed her mother around (though he did not physically beat her) and always got his way, while her mother meekly accepted being stepped on, did not stand up for herself (or her daughter), and saw herself as holding the family together through her ability to take punishment.

Thick boundaries sometimes appear as distance, coldness, and unwillingness to become involved. But thick interpersonal boundaries are also a sort of ideal taught to the child—in our culture, especially to the boy. For example, Kipling prescribes "If neither foe nor loving friend can hurt you" and "If all men count with you, but none too much" as the ideals that lead to "Yours is the earth and everything that's in it, and what is more, you'll be a man, my son" (Rudyard Kipling, "If").

BOUNDARIES BETWEEN CONSCIOUS AND UNCONSCIOUS AND BETWEEN ID, EGO, AND SUPEREGO

In the psychodynamic view of the mind, a great deal of the material found in the id—especially sexual and agressive impulses, childhood wishes, and the like—is kept unconscious, out of ordinary waking consciousness, by repression and other defense mechanisms. Thick boundaries in this sense imply strong repression; the unacceptable impulses are kept totally out of awareness. In people with thin boundaries there is less repression and less of a wall between id and ego, or unconscious and conscious. Such people are relatively aware of id material and allow themselves to think, daydream, and imagine all kinds of things—for instance, sexual relationships with members of both sexes or with members of their family—that others tend to repress. This type of boundary refers to *ego boundary* in the psychoanalytic sense.

In a person with thick boundaries, the superego appears to be very strong and sometimes very rigid or inflexible: "My life is full of 'shoulds,' " "My childhood was made up of 'You should do this' and 'You should do that'; now I do it to myself. I know just what I should do and I do it, automatically. I never really thought about it until we discussed it just now." The person with thick boundaries has solid introjects and/or solid identification, usually with the parent of the same sex. "I never noticed it, but people tell me I do things exactly the way my father did." Again, these examples only touch on a complex area that is related to the entire field of human psychodynamics.

DEFENSE MECHANISMS AS BOUNDARIES

The mechanisms of defense were conceptualized originally by Sigmund Freud and in more depth by Anna Freud (1946) as the ego's ways of handling (defending against) the sexual and aggressive drives of the id. The term is used in this way by psychoanalysts, but it is frequently expanded to include ways of defending oneself against danger from both internal and external sources. Anna Freud listed fourteen basic defense mechanisms; others have enlarged the list, and one authoritative source (Meissner 1985) now lists twenty-nine separate mechanisms.

A number of these defenses can be seen as boundaries, for they involve erecting some kind of barrier or wall. Repression, for example, sometimes called the most basic defense mechanism, involves walling off painful memories, keeping them out of awareness. Isolation involves keeping emotions walled off from thoughts. This mechanism again avoids pain; one can safely think all sorts of thoughts if one does not have to feel the associated emotions. Intellectualization, often associated with isolation, consists of putting up a wall of words and abstractions to avoid dealing wholly and emotionally with an issue.

The most pathological defense mechanism, seen mostly in psychotic patients but also in others at times of extreme stress such as just after the death of someone close, is denial. Here there is a wall between the self and the real world outside, a literal refusal to accept current reality that is too painful: "That just can't be so. It isn't so."

Identification is more than a defense, but it functions as a defense when one so totally identifies with another person—a parent, for instance—that one avoids the conflicts inherent in recognizing one's own wishes and making one's own decisions. One can ward off dangerous conflicts and painful decisions if one simply decides, without really thinking about it, that "this is the way Father did it, and it's the way I'm going to do it. Period."

Any of these defense mechanisms can be viewed as a type of boundary. A person with thick boundaries often use them more than a person with thin boundaries. It is not the case, however, that a person with thick boundaries will necessarily have more solid defenses in all these ways. Someone with very thick boundaries will often have one favorite defense among those described and will use it massively and almost constantly, usually without conscious awareness or intention. The person with thin boundaries will use these defenses less, or less consistently. Such a person often gives the impression of being "undefended."

THE BOUNDARIES OF IDENTITY

One's identity—the inner, not entirely conscious, sense of self—involves a number of important boundaries.

Sexual Identity

Sexual identity is itself a complex concept. At the center there is a core gender identity: does one basically think of oneself as male or female? In this basic sense, almost all the people I have interviewed, no matter how thick or thin their boundaries in other senses, have had a definite core gender identity. Surrounding this core, however, there are broader aspects of sexual identity and sexual preference, with a great deal of variation that may be related to boundary structure.

For example, people differ greatly in whether they sense themselves as being totally masculine or totally feminine or whether they accept some mixture, while keeping their core gender identity. Someone with thick boundaries in this sense considers the difference between men and women to be a given, an absolute fact of life. It's "us" and "them," not in a particularly antagonistic fashion, but just as a profound, unbridgeable gulf: "Who can tell what one of *them* is thinking?" For someone with a thick boundary, sexual identity is firm, absolute: "I'm a man; this is the way men do things. That's it. Women? Well, sure I like women; I love 'em, in fact, but they're so . . . so different!" This man is unlikely to imagine, or dream of, being a woman; he is likely to have difficulty seeing anything feminine in himself. Sigmund Freud was expressing his thick sexual identity (but also joking a bit) when he insisted on his inability to answer the basic question about a woman's motivation: "Wass will das Weib?" (What do women want?) A man with thinner boundaries will find it easier to recognize feminine as well as masculine parts of himself. He may have dreams or fantasies in which he is a woman.

There are also thick and thin boundaries in sexual preference, which is not the same as sexual identity. A man with thin boundaries in this sense may have dreams or fantasies in which he is having sex with a man or with a woman, or both. In my experience a person with very thin boundaries is not especially likely to be homosexual. In fact, some homosexuals who are quite definite in their sexual preference have thick boundaries in most senses. Rather the person with very thin boundaries is often bisexual, at least potentially. Such a person has fantasies, dreams, and daydreams of having sex with members of both sexes and is willing to consider the possibility of bisexual behavior, without necessarily acting on it.

Age Identity

An aspect of our identity that we consider less often is the age group of which we are a part—especially, for adults, the fact that we are now adults and not children. For some this is a solid, thick boundary: "I have put away the things of childhood." As we have seen, some of these people are unable even to remember much about their childhoods. For others—those with thinner boundaries—there is no such firm line; their childhood is still very much a part of them.

My impression is that at least some of those with thick boundaries have grown up more definitively and perhaps sooner than average. Some of them as children identified strongly with parents or older siblings and very much wanted to beome adult quickly. Once adult, they are happy with their new conditions and "slam the door behind them." In someone like this, adolescence may be fairly smooth—a simple matter of perfecting the adult role, with fewer of the conflicts produced by being a child, an adolescent, and an adult at the same time in the same body. Those with thin boundaries experience these conflicts of adolescence especially intensely.

Constancy of Identity

Yet another facet of identity is its constancy. On the one hand, one can think of one's identity as solid and fixed, unchanging over time or with circumstances, "constant as the northern star." Such a conception represents a thick boundary. On the other hand, one can see one's identity as flexible, changing over time or according to the situation: "I'm a totally different person when I'm with Tim." Such a person has a thin boundary in this sense.

GROUP BOUNDARIES

Invariably one experiences, or draws, a boundary around groups of which one is a part. The boundary can be thick and solid—one perceives a huge difference between "insiders" and "outsiders"— or thinner and more flexible. Group boundaries bear a relationship to one's identity as well. For some people, membership in a particular group is an extremely important part of their identity: "I am a Texan," "I am a Jewish professional," "I am an American." Obviously each of us is part of a group, in fact a part of many groups, but a thick boundary in this sense implies that being part of a specific group is an important part of being oneself;

one may act a certain way because "this is the way we Texans do things." If you hear a person with extremely thick boundaries in this sense talking about someone outside the group, it may sound as though a being of another species was being described.

Thick boundaries in this sense can also imply a strong sense of territoriality or "turf": "This is my block, my neighborhood; that's yours over there." Thick group boundaries also can show up as involvement with the rules and etiquette of a particular group or society. A person with very thick boundaries knows the rules well and goes along with them. Such a person may be seen as conventional.

Thin group boundaries imply a lack of the firm group distinctions just described. A person with thin boundaries will inevitably be part of various groups, but that fact will be a matter of relatively little importance. In terms of identity this person will not think of himself or herself as chiefly a member of some group but either as purely an individual (with fluctuating, casual group memberships) or as a member of a larger group without rigid boundaries, a "citizen of the world."

BOUNDARIES IN ORGANIZING ONE'S LIFE

Aside from the many internal "boundaries in the mind" but related to them are aspects of one's life style, preferences, and opinions that reflect thick or thin boundaries. These could be considered projections, styles of imposing internal boundaries on the outside world. (The group boundaries we have just discussed can likewise be considered a way of organizing one's life or imposing one's sense of boundaries on the world.)

Organization is a relatively simple aspect of boundaries. A person with thick boundaries often will want to have organized or well-bounded surroundings, believing in "a place for everything, and everything in its place." Such a person will usually have a neat desk and a functional house or apartment with well-defined spaces for each function or activity. One patient whom I saw over a long period always impressed me with his precision and organization. During our talks he would sometimes open his attaché case, which was divided into separate compartments precisely fitted for pens, pads, files, a calculator, and so on. There was never a loose pencil or scrap of paper, never a speck of dust. He would immediately lay his hands on the paper he wanted, read it or show it to me, file it back in its place, and snap the case shut. It seemed to me that his mind was much like his attaché case, or rather that he had organized his attaché case the way his mind was organized.

BOUNDARIES IN ENVIRONMENTAL PREFERENCES

Related to the liking for organization is a preference for thickness in actual physical boundaries in one's environment. The person with thick boundaries often prefers thick, solid clothing, heavy picture frames, and thick walls and doors. A man I saw in psychotherapy, who had one of the thickest scores on the Boundary Questionnaire, was having a new suburban house built for his family. He was proud of the plans he had drawn up with an architect and was especially happy that he had been able to order all doors to be 1 ⅛ inches thick instead of the usual ⅞ inch. Similarly, the person with thick boundaries prefers tightly structured situations, with definite rules and regulations: "In an organization everyone should have a clearly defined place and a specific role." Thin boundaries here imply a preference for less definite divisions in one's space, for less organization or looser organization, and for rules that are flexible or bendable.

Logically there is no reason why preferences in these areas should be related in a direct fashion to the various internal boundaries. There could be an opposite relationship (negative correlation) or no relationship at all. Among the people I have studied, in fact, there were some who had one specific type of opposite relationship: some who had very thin internal boundaries, in the sense of feeling fragile and vulnerable, tried to compensate at certain times by surrounding themselves with thick walls and well-structured organizations (see chapter 10). These were the exceptions, however. Most people appear to prefer to find their style of internal boundaries in the world or to impose them on the world.

BOUNDARIES IN OPINIONS AND JUDGMENTS

Thick boundaries imply definite, firm divisions between categories and concepts. People with very thick boundaries approve of statements such as "East is East and West is West, and never the twain shall meet" (Kipling); "A man is a man; a woman is a woman; vive la différence!"; and "Either you're sane or you're crazy; there's no in-between." In other words thick boundaries in this sense involve a tendency to see blacks and whites, with little gray in between. People with thin boundaries will tend to see everything in shades of gray.

Within the major philosophical categories—the nature of the real (metaphysics), the beautiful (esthetics), and the good (ethics)—or at least in our judgments about them, there are definite boundaries, and there is a thick and a thin position. People with thick boundaries will tend to believe that there are definite criteria or rules determining what is real, what is beautiful, and what is good. They will have definite, unchangeable standards and will consider themselves to have solid judgment and a firm morality immune to passing whims or fashions. People with thin boundaries are more likely to say, "It all depends."

BOUNDARIES IN DECISION MAKING AND ACTION

Action and decision making can be considered the output of the system. After one has perceived the world, taken in information in a certain style, processed the information, and formed preferences or opinions in a certain style, one then takes, or does not take, action. Someone who has thick boundaries in the categories we have just discussed—someone who has a definite sense of organization, has definite categorical opinions, and knows what's right or what's best—will find it relatively easy to make a decision, take an action, and then go on to something else. Someone with the opposite characteristics, who sees shades of gray and can appreciate all sides of an issue, may find it much harder to make a decision and take action.

This chapter should have conveyed a sense of what I mean by the different types of boundaries in the mind and the broad sense in which I am using the term *boundary.* Examples have been taken from real people, but they have been chosen for purposes of emphasis. In order to highlight the differences, I have often indicated what someone with extremely thick or extremely thin boundaries might do or say or prefer; most people fall somewhere in between, and many of us have thick aspects and thin aspects, so that we do not think or act consistently in one way or the other.

CHAPTER 3

Predecessors of the Boundary Concept

THE CONCEPT of thin and thick boundaries has not to my knowledge been previously used as I am using it—that is, as a broad dimension of personality and an aspect of the overall organization of the mind. It has a number of precursors, however, in conceptualizations that capture at least a part of what we are discussing.

William James (1907) discussed at length two types of what he called *temperament.* He believed that "the history of philosophy is to a great extent that of a certain clash of human temperaments" (p.6) and went on to describe two principal temperaments, which he called *rationalist* and *empiricist.* The rationalist temper, which he also called *tender-minded,* he described as "starting from whole or universals, making much of the unity of things" (p.9). The tender-minded are "idealistic, optimistic, religious, free-willist, monistic, dogmatical" (p.9).

The empiricists, on the other hand, also called the

tough-minded, are described as "starting from the parts," not the whole, and "going by facts." They are "materialistic, pessimistic, irreligious, fatalistic, pluralistic, sceptical" (p.9). James emphasized that few thinkers are pure examples of the two types—most are mixtures—but he saw these temperaments as two general tendencies in human thinking.

There certainly appears to be a relationship between James's temperaments and our concept of boundaries. At least in relation to styles of thinking about the world—the boundaries pertaining to organization, preferences, and opinions—the tough-minded empiricists definitely have thick boundaries and the tender-minded rationalists have thin boundaries.

One prominent theorist who used the concept of boundaries more explicitly was Kurt Lewin (1935, 1936). He diagrammed the mind as divided into a number of regions or "psychical systems" acting upon each other and separated from each other by lines of different thickness. For example, he states,

> The structure of the dynamic system involved and the presence (in greater or lesser degree) or the absence of communication with various other psychical systems, as well as every change in boundary conditions, are of the greatest significance for the psychical process, for the equilibration of psychical tensions, and for the flow of psychical energy. (1935, p. 62)

Certainly Lewin is discussing an aspect of what I call boundaries in the mind.

Sigmund Freud made only a few explicit references to

boundaries, most notably to what he called the *Reizschutz,* a protective shield, or barrier against stimulation. He considered the *Reizschutz* to be an important part of all organisms, even primitive unicellular creatures (1923). In *Inhibitions, Symptoms, and Anxiety* (1925) he discussed intense outbreaks of anxiety in children, which then lead to repression. "It is highly likely that the immediate precipitating causes of primal repressions are quantitative factors such as an excessive degree of excitation and the breaking through of the protective shield against stimuli" (p. 94). In *Beyond the Pleasure Principle* (1920), he noted, "We describe as traumatic the excitations from outside which are powerful enough to break through the protective shield" (p. 29).

Aside from his many discussions of the *Reizschutz,* Freud did not speak of boundaries in the specific senses I have discussed in chapter 2. He was very aware of the importance of boundaries, however, and the concept of boundaries is implicit in much of his work. He referred to the entire ego as initially a *body ego,* derived from the body surface (1923). The concept of boundaries around the ego is also involved in Freud's many discussions of the ego's defending itself or protecting itself from the id and from the outside world. This aspect of defensive boundaries is considered in great detail by David Rapaport (1960).

Freud himself did not use the term *ego boundary,* but some of his followers, especially Paul Federn, use it extensively to refer to the boundary or division between ego and id, ego and superego, and ego and outside world. Federn elaborates on the concept in great clinical detail in his work on psychosis (1952). His view is that the basic difference between the healthy individual and the psychotic one is that the healthy person knows intuitively what is inside and what is outside himself or herself, what is fantasy and what is reality, whereas the person prone to psychosis has incompletely formed boundaries and has great trouble in making these distinctions. It is the lack of these basic distinctions that leads to the many kinds of psychotic pathology. The term *ego boundary* is in fact used quite widely in the psychoanalytic literature in this sense and often in a broader sense as well; poorly formed ego boundaries or permeable ego boundaries are often mentioned in describing severe psychopathology. As we saw in the last chapter, this is certainly an important aspect of what we mean by boundaries.

Extending the work of Freud and Federn, the French psychoanalyst Didier Anzieu (1987) has recently developed the concept of an *ego-skin (moi-peau)*, a complex envelope for the ego that is derived from the baby's early experience of a common skin between itself and its mother. The ego-skin is conceptualized as performing all the functions for the ego that the skin performs for the body. This concept is certainly related to our discussion of boundaries. Anzieu approaches the concept of individual differences in boundaries in his references to the unusually solid or thick ego-skin of narcissistic people and the wounded ego-skin of masochistic people.

The many psychoanalysts and other clinicians who write of ego boundaries have made no attempt to quantify or measure the permeability of boundaries or other aspects of boundaries. Such attempts have been made, however, by Rorschach psychologists working within the psychoanalytic tradition. The Rorschach test is the well-known projective test in which the subject is asked to describe what he or she sees in each of ten standard inkblots. Among the many types of scoring devised for the Rorschach are two scales that relate specifically to boundaries. Sidney Blatt and his associates (Blatt and Ritzler 1974; Blatt et al. 1976) developed a scoring system for permeable ego boundaries or boundary deficit, based on the number of responses that involve "contamination," "fabulized combination," or "confabulation"; these are unusual responses to the inkblots, in which the subject fuses two different percepts or sees several things merged or in strange combinations ("men with big donkeys' heads") or generalizes from a small detail to make up a fantasy that seems unrelated to the inkblot as a whole. Clearly Blatt's group is studying what we would call thin boundaries, but with an emphasis on the pathological aspects; the people who score high on Blatt's scale are often psychotic or close to psychotic.

Fisher and Cleveland (1968) started from a different point of view. They were interested in body image, including the sense of body limits or body boundary. They developed two Rorschach measures: *barrier,* composed of the number of times the subject sees images such as walls, armor, and animals with heavy scales or fur, to measure body boundary solidity, and *penetration,* the sum of images such as torn skin or clothing and thin or transparent elements, to measure body boundary fragility. Fisher and Cleveland were not studying psychopathology as such, but they examined a range of relationships between their scales and skin disease, psychosomatic illness of various kinds, and occupation. They noted some interesting results, especially with the *barrier* score. High barrier scores turned out to be correlated with lower incidence of several kinds of illness as well as with self-confidence and success in a number of situations.

Several of Fisher and Cleveland's findings are somewhat surprising. Penetration scores were not negatively correlated with barrier scores; there was no relationship between them, and it was less clear to what penetration scores might be related. Also, barrier and penetration scores can change rapidly; for example, barrier scores increase after exercise and after rubbing the skin. Apparently barrier measures an awareness of one's skin or body surface that is not necessarily an enduring feature of personality. Finally, Fisher and Cleveland's scores do not seem to be measuring the same thing as Blatt's scale; the two measures show a zero correlation with each other. (For a review of these studies, see Fisher 1986.)

A psychologist in our group, Ilana Sivan, developed a detailed Rorschach scale of boundary permeability (which we would now call "thin boundaries") and boundary defense (1983), based on both Blatt's and Fisher's work. These measures were used in our original groups of people with nightmares, who turned out to score especially high on the boundary permeability measure. This Rorschach measure has not as yet been widely used.

These various Rorschach scales obviously relate in some way to our own interests, but they do not relate well with one another. And they are not necessarily measuring a long-term personality trait. An additional problem with the Rorschach test is that it must be administered by a psychologist trained in the specific technique and often requires three hours or more to administer and score. Furthermore, there is considerable room for disagreement in scoring and interpretation, so that interrater reliability is not always high. It was these considerations, as noted in chapter 1, that pointed to the need for a simpler and more reliable measure and led to the development of the Boundary Questionnaire.

Bernard Landis has written a monograph (1970) in which he started with the psychoanalytic concept of ego boundaries and tried to develop tests to measure their permeability and impermeability. His concept of ego boundaries was broader than the narrow definition involving the ego's boundary with the id and the superego; he may have been thinking of boundaries in something like the broad sense I am discussing here.

Landis's tests were ingenious. In one test the subject was given an unframed picture on paper and asked to draw a frame around it. The frames were then judged for such features as solidity, width, completeness, and number of gaps, which gave a score of permeability or impermeability. In another test the subject was asked to place several stick figures on an empty page, and the result was rated for closeness or distance between figures, as a measure of interpersonal boundaries.

These measures do not appear to have been used by others to any extent, at least in part because Landis did not obtain clear-cut results with his tests; the scores of his "permeable" group were only slightly different from those of his "impermeable" group. I believe that the problem was not that the tests are seriously flawed but rather that his groups were chosen from among his colleagues and students, so that he had a very limited range of subjects. His tests might well discriminate among some of the more clear-cut "thin" or "thick" groups we have studied.

These are the principal concepts and measures that relate most directly to our work with thick and thin boundaries. There are many others that might also be relevant to some aspects of boundaries. I have already alluded to the fact that many of the defense mechanisms discussed in psychoanalytic theory, such as repression and isolation, are examples of boundaries of a certain kind, and of course these are discussed widely in the psychoanalytic literature. In addition, Gardner and his colleagues (1959), in their work on cognitive controls, introduce a measure of cognitive style that they call "category width": how many diverse objects a person can tolerate as belonging to the same category. A large category width means a relaxing of conceptual boundaries between the objects and can be seen as an aspect of thin boundaries.

Carl Gustav Jung did not write specifically about boundaries, but he initiated a great deal of work on personality in his *Psychological Types* (1921). Although his basic dichotomy between extroverts and introverts does not appear related to boundaries, his typology involving preference for different modes of cognition—thinking, feeling, sensing, and intuiting—bears at least some relationship with boundaries. We are currently attempting to study the relationship of more recent quantifications of Jung's typology, the Myers-Briggs type indicator (Myers 1962), with our boundary measures.

Many psychotherapists employ the term *boundary* in

one way or another. Family therapists in particular make use of the concept in terms of interpersonal boundaries; they speak of boundaries between family members, generational boundaries, boundaries around the family, boundary violations, and so on (see for instance Kanter and Lehr 1975).

Thus the concept of boundaries is not new. Many aspects of the types of boundaries discussed in the last chapter have been investigated and used in various ways. In the next chapter I discuss in greater detail the new measure introduced in chapter 1, the Boundary Questionnaire, which has been designed specifically to measure thick and thin boundaries in the broad sense we have been discussing.

CHAPTER 4

Measuring Boundaries

THE BOUNDARY QUESTIONNAIRE

Based on our previous work with people who had frequent nightmares, and on other interview studies as well, I felt that much of the information about a person's boundaries which we had painstakingly developed from interviews and projective tests could probably be obtained more simply by the use of a questionnaire. The Boundary Questionnaire was designed to include questions about all the types of boundaries discussed in the last chapters.

The Boundary Questionnaire as finally tested and standardized, is reproduced on pages 80–93. It consists of 145 items, divided into twelve categories.

1. Sleep/wake/dream (14 items)

   EXAMPLE When I awake in the morning, I am not sure whether I am really awake for a few minutes.

2. Unusual experiences (19 items)
   EXAMPLE I have had déjà vu experiences.

3. Thoughts, feeling, moods (16 items)
   EXAMPLE Sometimes I don't know whether I am thinking or feeling.

4. Childhood, adolescence, adulthood (6 items)
   EXAMPLE I am very close to my childhood feelings.

5. Interpersonal (15 items)
   EXAMPLE When I get involved with someone, we sometimes get too close.

6. Sensitivity (5 items)
   EXAMPLE I am very sensitive to other people's feelings.

7. Neat, exact, precise (11 items)
   EXAMPLE I keep my desk or worktable neat and well organized.

8. Edges, lines, clothing (20 items)
   EXAMPLE I like houses with flexible spaces, where you can shift things around and make different uses of the same rooms.

9. Opinions about children and others (8 items)
   EXAMPLE I think a good teacher must remain in part a child.

10. Opinions about organizations (10 items)
    EXAMPLE In an organization, everyone should have a definite place and a specific role.

11. Opinions about people, nations, groups (14 items)
    EXAMPLE There are no sharp dividing lines between normal people, people with problems, and people who are considered psychotic or crazy.

12. Opinions about beauty, truth (7 items)
    EXAMPLE Either you are telling the truth or you are lying; that's all there is to it.

Within each category, items cover as wide a range as possible. For example, in the first category, Sleep/wake/dream, there are items about sleep-wake boundaries ("When I wake up, I wake up quickly and I am absolutely sure I am awake"); about dreams ("In my dreams, people sometimes merge into each other or become other people"); about dreams and waking ("My dreams are so vivid that even later I can't tell them from waking reality"); about daydreams ("My daydreams don't always stay in control"); and about a number of in-between experiences ("I spend a lot of time daydreaming, fantasizing, or in reverie").

Subjects are instructed to respond to each item on a five-point scale from 0 *(no, not at all,* or *not at all true of me)* to 4 (*yes, definitely,* or *definitely true of me).* About two-thirds of the items are worded so that 4 is thinnest (for example, "I feel unsure of who I am at times"); one-third are worded in the opposite direction, so that 4 is thickest and 0 is thinnest (for example, "I have friends and I have enemies, and I know which are which"). In scoring the questionnaire, the scores on the items measuring thinness are added directly; the scores on the items measuring thickness are first inverted (0 = 4, 1 = 3, and so on) and then added.

Each person receives a subscore on each of the twelve categories, a total score for the first eight categories (called the *Personal Total*), a total for the last four categories (called the *World Total*), and an overall total boundary score *(SumBound).* High scores always correspond to thinness. The entire Boundary Questionnaire and score sheet appears on pages 80–95.

A preliminary version of the Boundary Questionnaire was taken by thirty colleagues and students, who were asked not only to respond to the items but also to comment on any ambiguity or lack of clarity in the wording. On the basis of these preliminary results, we discussed each item, reworded a number of them, and produced the basic 145-item Boundary Questionnaire that appears at the end of this chapter.

On the basis of the results in the first eight hundred persons who took the Boundary Questionnaire, a further refinement was made. Most of the individual questions correlated well—very positively—with the total score (SumBound). Seven of the 145 items, however, correlated at a level of zero, or even slightly negatively. My notes revealed that these seven were items about whose wording we had not been entirely satisfied. It was therefore decided not to include these seven items in the data analysis. Although all 145 items are filled out by each subject who takes the Boundary Questionnaire, the data analysis is actually based on 138 items.

What follows here are some of our basic findings about the internal structure of the test and the results with some special groups, based on the data analysis for the first 866 people who took it. Further results with these and other subjects relating to differences between men and women, different occupational groups, artists of different kinds, healthy and ill subjects, and other distinctions will be discussed in later chapters.

About half the total group of 866 were unselected students; the other half were patients or research subjects studied for specific reasons. For example, to check on whether the Boundary Questionnaire measured what we thought it was measuring (face validity), we included several groups of people who we predicted a priori would score much thinner than average. These were two new groups of nightmare sufferers and two groups of art students. We also studied one group of line naval officers who we predicted a priori would have thick boundaries.

First we tested the questionnaire for internal reliability, using a computer technique that allows the questionnaire to be split into halves in all possible ways and then compares the two halves. This measure, called the Cronbach Alpha, came out as .930, which is very high and indicates that the test is reliable in this sense.

To examine further the internal structure of the test, Robert Harrison in our group performed an exploratory factor analysis using principal components extraction. This procedure, applied to a large body of data, reveals which questions correlate with which other questions and what patterns are formed. The results of a factor analysis are often surprising: one finds things that one did not realize were there, and often there are uninterpretable results. In this case, the best solution of the factor analysis produced thirteen factors, and we were pleased to note that almost all (the first twelve of the thirteen) were easily interpretable as aspects of thin or thick boundaries. In other words, the factors made sense in terms of our original conception of boundaries and also in terms of clinical descriptions and formulations.

For example, the first and most solid factor refers to primary process thinking. It describes vivid imagery, fluctuating identity, and experiences of merging of different kinds. Factor I turns out to include many of the questions in our original categories 1 (sleep/wake/dream), 2 (unusual experiences), and 3 (thoughts, feelings, moods). The second most solid factor deals not with personal experience but with a preference for clear borders: in relationships, in stories, in houses, in groups of people, and so on. Many of the items included in factor II are those in categories 10 and 11, involving opinions. Factor III was clearly related to identification with children—such items as "I am very close to my childhood feelings" and "A good teacher needs to remain in part a child." Factor IV was related to fragility or vulnerability. A complete listing of the thirteen factors in the factor analysis of the Boundary Questionnaire is found in table 2. We were encouraged to find that what came out of the questionnaire in the factor analysis corresponded quite closely to what we thought should have been in it and was also closely related to the major types of boundaries discussed in chapter 2.

We also examined the validity of the Boundary Ques-

Table 2 Summary of Factor Analysis ($N = 866$)

Factor I Primary Process Thinking. The 51 items in this factor (all keyed in the thin boundary direction) describe a person who has many experiences of merging and of fluctuating identity; whose imagery is so vivid it is hard to distinguish from reality; who experiences synesthesia; the merging of objects with self and with each other. Theta reliability = .92.

Factor II Preference for Explicit Boundaries.* The 37 items in this factor (36 keyed in the thick boundary direction) express a preference for clear borders whether it is in nations, cities, houses, pictures, stories, or relationships. A secondary emphasis is on neatness. Theta = .87.

Factor III Identification with Children. The 19 items in this factor (18 keyed thin) describe a person who feels, in part, like a child; identifies with children and enjoys them. Theta = .75.

Factor IV Fragility. The 13 items in this factor (12 keyed thin) express sensitivity to hurt, a difficult and complicated childhood and adolescence, fears of falling apart, and fears of being overwhelmed by interpersonal involvement. Theta = .75.

Factor V Percipience/Clairvoyance. The 16 items on this factor (14 keyed thin) include beliefs in one's clairvoyant powers including knowing others' unexpressed thoughts and feelings, having premonitory dreams, and experiencing very vivid memories and imagery. These items also suggest a strong sense of self-identity from childhood through old age. Theta = .70.

Factor VI Trustful Openness. The 11 items on this factor (all keyed thin) describe a person who believes in being open to the world, trusting others, and disclosing personal experience. Theta = .70.

Factor VII Organized Planfulness.* The 15 items on this factor (all keyed thick) describe a well-organized, methodical, planful person who keeps track of everything. Theta = .67.

Table 2 (*Continued*)

Factor VIII Belief in Impenetrable Intergroup Boundaries.* The 10 items on this factor (all keyed thick) describe a person who believes in intergroup segregation whether a group is defined by nationality, race, age, or gender. Theta = .65.

Factor IX Flexibility. The 12 items (10 keyed thin) in this factor have four themes: those of wishing to shape one's own space, job, life; recognizing separateness in close relationships (2 items); appreciating without analyzing (2 items); and believing that people are more the same than they are different. Theta = .57.

Factor X Overinvolvement in Fantasy. The six items in this factor (all keyed thin) are concerned with the difficulty of making transitions from one state to another—whether it is from being asleep to being awake, from listening to music or playing a game to ordinary states of consciousness. Theta = .57.

Factor XI Preference for Simple Geometric Forms.* The five items in this factor (all keyed thick) describe a person who likes straight lines, and would like to work as a navigator or an engineer. Theta = .56.

Factor XII Isolation of Affect.* Two of the five items in this factor (all keyed thick) describe a person who explicitly believes in the segregation of thinking from feeling and favors rationality over emotion. Theta = .56.

*In this table, these factors are interpreted in their 'natural' (positive loadings are keyed true) direction.

tionnaire by checking whether groups we had predicted would be especially thin (the art students and nightmare sufferers) or especially thick (the naval officers) did indeed score that way. These predictions were very strongly supported. The predicted thin groups scored significantly higher (thinner) than the predicted thick group at high levels of significance ($p < .0001$), not only for the total boundary score SumBound but for the two subtotals, Personal Total and World Total. The predicted thin groups also scored significantly higher on all the individual categories and on six of the factors (see Appendix, table A-1). We concluded that the Boundary Questionnaire has face validity: the results confirmed what we had predicted about these groups on the basis of other information such as interviews and previous studies of similar groups.

It was interesting that the thin groups differed among themselves on the important factor IV, fragility. The art students scored approximately as high (thin) on the overall test as did the nightmare sufferers, but nightmare sufferers were considerably more fragile in the sense of high scores on factor IV. This again is consistent with our knowledge of the groups.

Overall, we found that women scored slightly but consistently thinner than men on the Boundary Questionnaire. We also found that the older subjects in our sample scored somewhat thicker than younger subjects. Both of these relationships will be discussed further in a later chapter. The Appendix includes further data on the Boundary Questionnaire.

THE VERY THICK AND THE VERY THIN: TWO GROUP PORTRAITS

What do thick and thin scores on the Boundary Questionnaire really mean? What is it like to have really thick boundaries or really thin boundaries? We will first look at group profiles of twenty persons who scored very thick and twenty who scored very thin, and then consider two individual case studies.

The first 866 people who took the Boundary Questionnaire were sorted by computer and listed according to their total boundary score (SumBound). I then went back to whatever records were available to determine the characteristics of those who scored at the two extremes. The overall mean SumBound was 273 +/− 52; all of those selected for closer study scored more than one and one-half standard deviations above or below the mean (above 351 or below 195). Since little or no information was available on the student groups, what follows is based chiefly on patients—especially patients seen at a sleep disorder center—and people taking part in research studies.

The group of twenty people who scored thickest, for whom information was available, turned out to consist of six women and fourteen men, with a mean age of fifty-one (older than most of our subjects). All of them were married; surprisingly, not a single member of this group was single, divorced, or widowed at the time they filled out the questionnaire. Their occupations were skewed toward business, law, and engineering: six were business executives or managers, two were sales representatives working for large companies, three were lawyers, and three were engineers. There were also three homemakers, one architect, one electrician, and one technician. The group did not contain a single teacher, health or human services worker, or anyone connected with the arts. All had been asked about nightmares and about other dreams. They all reported either no nightmares or fewer than one nightmare per year. Interestingly, most also said they dreamed rarely and found it hard to recall a detailed dream.

In psychological terms they all could be described as fairly normal and fairly conventional. Most of them had average scores on all the clinical scales of the MMPI (see chapter 5). They also scored in the normal range on a symptom checklist called the Cornell Index (Weider et al. 1944). They were solid citizens; most of them could be called hardworking and hard-driving, and some could be called perfectionistic.

Only two of the twenty could be given a psychiatric diagnosis using the standard DSM-IIIR criteria,* in neither case a true clinical disorder. In both cases the diagnosis was obsessive-compulsive personality disorder; the subjects had in especially clear form the characteristics spelled out as "preoccupation with rules, efficiency, trivial details, procedures or form [that] interferes with the ability to take a broad view of things" (p. 354). Three others had some features of obsessive-compulsive personality disorder, but not enough to make a diagnosis. The others had no trace of any psychiatric condition. A number of the subjects had been seen as patients with sleep disorders, but as we will see in chapter 8, they turned out to have organic sleep disorders such as sleep apnea or nocturnal myoclonus; their sleep disorders were not the result of psychiatric problems.

The twenty thinnest scorers on whom information is available were a very different group. There were seventeen women and only three men, and the average age

*DSM-IIIR is the newest version of the diagnostic manual referred to in chapter 1. This version was not available when the original studies of nightmares were performed.

was 36. Of the nineteen for whom marital status is recorded, twelve were single, six were married, and one was divorced.

Their occupations were also very different from those of the thick scorers. Four of the group were homemakers, three were teachers, two were artists, and the rest were one of a kind—one nurse, one laborer, one counselor, and so on. It is of interest that this group included no lawyers, no engineers, and no business executives, although it was drawn from the same population as the thick group.

Recall of dreams was high in this thin-boundary group. Most remembered dreams almost every night, and the majority reported having at least some nightmares—in three cases one or more nightmares per week.

Psychologically these subjects were very different from the thick-boundary group. None of them struck the interviewers as conventional, hard-driven, or perfectionistic. Although they differed greatly among themselves, terms that recurred in the descriptions about them included "sensitive," "fragile," "schizotypal," and "history of a suicide attempt."

Psychological tests, where available, showed varying degrees of psychopathology. Many of these people had high scores (two standard deviations above normal means) on at least some of the clinical scales of the MMPI. The scales most often elevated in members of the group were Sc (schizophrenia) and Pa (paranoia). This does not mean that they could be diagnosed as clinically schizophrenic or paranoid; the MMPI scores merely indicate that the subjects answered a variety of true/false questions in the same directions as patients with these diagnoses. In fact it is well known that high Sc scores are characteristic of artists as well as people with several of the personality disorders, and high Pa scores are frequently found in people who are considered interpersonally sensitive (Dahlstrom et al. 1972; Graham 1977).

Eleven of the twenty could be given a psychiatric diagnosis. In four cases it was schizotypal personality disorder, spelled out in DSM-IIIR as "magical thinking . . . a sense that others can feel my feelings," and "recurrent illusions: sensing the presence of a force or person not actually present" (p. 340). One subject had a definite diagnosis of borderline personality disorder, and three others were diagnosed mixed personality disorder, including features of borderline personality disorder, specifically "a pattern of unstable and intense interpersonal relationships, e.g. marked shifts of attitude [or] idealization" and "identity disturbances, manifested by several issues related to identity, such as gender identity, long-term goals or career choice, friendship patterns, values and loyalties" (p. 346).

One member of the group had a diagnosis of schizophrenia, one generalized anxiety disorder, and one dysthymic disorder (a chronic tendency to depression). Five of the twenty definitely had no psychiatric diagnosis, and in four cases there was not enough information to make a decision.

It must be kept in mind that the thin group, like the thick group, came from a population including patients complaining of sleep disorders. Thus the differences between these people and the thick group are impressive, but one cannot conclude that a group with thin boundaries chosen from the population at large would show as much pathology. Obviously there was considerable psychopathology in this thin group, although the diagnosis was usually a personality disorder rather than a true illness or "clinical disorder."

Moreover, those with sleep disorders in this thin-scoring group mostly had insomnia related to psychiatric disorder, rather than one of the organic sleep disorders. Clearly there were many differences between the two extreme-scoring groups in terms of occupation, life style, and personality features. Due to the nature of our sample, both groups included people with sleep disorders; therefore, the data on frequency of insomnia and other sleep disorders cannot be expected to hold in the general population.

TWO CASE STUDIES

I am in the fortunate position of being able to combine data obtained from two very different sources: the questionnaire technique, in which a small amount of information is obtained on a large number of people, about whom one usually knows nothing beyond their answers on a particular questionnaire, and the very different method of long-term individual psychotherapy and psychoanalysis, which can be considered just the opposite in that one learns a huge amount about a very few people. For a time I routinely asked new patients to fill out the Boundary Questionnaire. Thus I have questionnaire scores as well as detailed personal information from psychotherapy on a number of patients. Several of these patients scored either at the extreme thin end or the extreme thick end of the Boundary Questionnaire. I will present two brief case studies here, one from each end of the boundary continuum, disguised to protect confidentiality.

Heather, the woman who scored extremely thin, is twenty-eight years old, unmarried, and lives alone most of the time. She has had several long but stormy relationships with men and has considered marriage several times. She works as a music teacher, and she is also a talented musical performer and composer.

She came to see me initially because of terrifying nightmares and anxiety, but it quickly became clear that she also wanted help in understanding herself and in organizing her life, which often felt out of control. She described herself as having been a bright child, but in some turmoil or pain for much of her life. Her family and her childhood environment sound fairly average on the surface. The third of four children, she grew up in an intact family, with no known traumatic events. She was never abused or physically deserted by her parents, but she does describe her mother as sometimes depressed, and often unable to provide comfort when she needed it.

What Heather remembers most is that she was always extremely sensitive, so that things hurt her that might have had less effect on others. She would hurt for herself and hurt for others too. She says, "I couldn't keep things out; everything got to me all the time." For example, when she found a rabbit injured by a passing car she was inconsolable and could not get the picture of the suffering rabbit out of her mind for days. Her brothers would take advantage of her sensitivity by pretending to hurt an animal or by talking about killing animals, just to get her upset. In fact she became a lifelong vegetarian, chiefly because she could not bear the idea of anyone killing an animal so that others could eat it. Likewise, whenever her parents argued, she took their conflict extremely seriously and felt sure they were about to be divorced.

She performed well academically, took part in athletics at times, and found it easy to make friends at school, but nonetheless she considered herself an outsider. She felt that her intense artistic interests as well as her sensitivity set her apart. She was sometimes jealous of the most popular kids, whose lives seemed to go so smoothly, but just as often she felt superior to them: more perceptive, more caring, more aware of the cruelty of the world around her.

Heather's adolescence and early adulthood were stormy, with a number of intense friendships and a few love affairs, which often ended with feelings of rejection followed by severe depressions, on one occasion so severe that she made a suicide attempt. There was also one brief episode of psychosis, during which she lost touch with reality and had hallucinations for two days; it occurred at a time when she was using marijuana and several other drugs, with which she experimented from adolescence on, although she never became truly addicted to any of them. She has seen several psychiatrists for brief psychotherapy, which she feels did not produce much change. And she has taken antidepressant medication, which helped her recover from her most serious episode of depression.

Despite these problems, when she came to see me she was alert and charming, not particularly depressed, and she was enjoying life in many ways. She loved music and was very much involved in it; she genuinely liked teaching children; she appreciated nature deeply—she could become engrossed for hours in the interplay of sand and water on the beach—and she definitely enjoyed sex.

Working with Heather in therapy was fascinating but also very difficult. It was fascinating because she was so bright and always had a lot to say. She found the basic rule of psychoanalysis and psychoanalytic therapy—say whatever comes to mind—extremely easy and congenial. She always had things to talk about, became intrigued by them, and was led on to other related topics. In other words she found it very easy to free-associate but hard to stop and learn from what she had been saying.

What made therapy difficult, apart from her very casual attitude about time and money (she frequently came late or missed appointments completely, and she seldom paid her bills), was that she was unable to focus on one aspect of her life at a time and try to understand it and make changes. Rather she was always being pulled off onto interesting tangents, and everything seemed to be of equal importance to her. For example, she would come in to tell me of interesting dreams or daydreams or ideas for her work, while I had to keep reminding her that she was still involved with a completely inappropriate boyfriend with whom she'd fallen desperately in love but who had beaten her up several times already and might very well kill her in one of his drug-induced rages. It was obvious to me, but apparently not to her, that it was essential for her to deal with this situation quickly. In fact it was clear to me that learning to set limits (thicken her boundaries) in this particular area of personal relationships was of the utmost importance to her life.

Heather was able to make some progress in understanding and changing her dangerous behaviors (she did give up the boyfriend). She was very intuitive in therapy and experienced dramatic insights or "a-ha experiences." And she made use of bits of transference material, using her therapeutic relationship with me to understand her relationship with her parents. She discontinued therapy, however, before more solid changes had occurred. I have not seen her for three years; I am curious as to how she is doing and a bit worried about her.

Charles, a man who scores extremely thick, is also very intelligent. He is a successful forty-year-old businessman who enjoys good relations with his colleagues and employees. Married and the father of three children, he lives in a large house in the suburbs on six acres of land; he enjoys having plenty of space around him.

He first came to see me for a sleep problem, which appeared to have a physical cause and for which he wanted a straightforward physical treatment. He had tried several medications in the past, but they were not of great help. I told him that physical treatments might help but that I also believed his condition had psychological components, and I suggested psychotherapy. He wanted to try any available physical treatments first; only when these proved of little help did he agree to try psychotherapy for a time.

Charles's childhood was spent in an intact, religious, well-functioning family. He did not experience any obvious traumatic events. A striking feature of his therapy is that although this man has an excellent memory for the recent past, he remembers almost nothing specific from before the age of nine, although eventually he has recalled a few events. The memories he does have present a picture of a solid, somewhat rigid family with a strong father and, in the background, a strong grandfather who was also an important figure in Charles's childhood. Charles remembers a few pearls of wisdom from his father and his grandfather that he treasures and enjoys retelling. The theme is usually related to self-reliance: "Give a man a fish and you feed him for a day; teach him how to fish and you feed him for a lifetime."

A brother two years older played an important role in Charles's early life. The dominant theme for Charles was to try to grow up fast so that he could be just as big, smart, and adult as his brother and, if possible, to surpass him.

His intelligence as well as his liking for organization helped him academically, and he did very well in school and in college. He had several good friends in college and one girlfriend in his senior year, but the impression he conveys is that emotional experiences and relationships have never played a major role in his life. Thus, although he interacts with a great many people in his work and in his many civic and church activities, he says, "My only friend is my wife." And he notes that although he and his wife get along fine, he does not feel very close even to her. They lead active but in a sense separate, parallel lives. This man is very aware of himself as representing his class and his religious group. He "lives up to standards" and feels that rules and regulations are a very important part of life.

I have worked with Charles in psychotherapy for two years. In many ways he seems to be the opposite of Heather. He is a wonderful patient in the sense that he makes appointments and never forgets them. He is absolutely punctual, and he always pays his bills. Working with Charles in therapy is difficult, however, because he finds it extremely hard to free-associate. He wants me to ask him specific questions to which he can give specific answers. He wants to have a sense of completion; he does not enjoy being involved in open-ended discussions, and at first it was very hard for him to talk about his feelings. He speaks in a precise, clipped manner; interestingly, the muscles of his face and body also appear precisely arranged and somewhat rigid. When he occasionally does laugh or smile broadly, it takes a while for the laugh to appear on his face, as though his facial muscles are unused to it, and then there is an abrupt loosening; the expression "break into a smile" describes the process quite literally.

Charles likes to view life from a mechanical or an engineering point of view. When he has a problem, he looks for a specific and if possible mechanical solution. On one occasion he showed me a photograph in which he is frowning, with the corners of his mouth turned down. He said, "I don't like that frown. Do you think I should get plastic surgery to have the corners of my mouth turned up?"

In some ways this man can be called an obsessive-compulsive person, but he does not fully meet the criteria for any psychiatric diagnosis, not even obsessive-compulsive personality disorder. By most definitions he is a very healthy person, well adjusted to society. His scores are absolutely normal—in the midrange of normal scores, in fact—on all scales of the MMPI. His only unusual test score is his very thick overall score on the Boundary Questionnaire.

Charles's psychotherapy has progressed slowly but steadily. My emphasis is on helping him become "looser" and allowing him to see more of his emotional life, his fantasies, and his dreams, which previously appear to have been pushed away or walled off. At the beginning he almost never remembered a dream, nor did he have fantasies or daydreams. When he did start to dream, the first dream he remembered well involved being in a small room inside the works of a huge dam, so that he was surrounded by heavy concrete on three sides, with one open side through which he could look out. This struck me as a "self-state dream" that accurately portrayed a part of his psychological self. A number of his dreams in fact involve walls and fences of various kinds, but over time his dreams have become more complex and varied.

Nothing very dramatic has occurred in therapy. His sleep condition has improved only slightly, but he does feel that psychotherapy has been broadening, has helped him get to know himself better, and perhaps has helped with his personal relationships. Unlike Heather, he does not make wild imaginative leaps or have sudden a-ha experiences, but when he does see something new or in a new way, he holds on to the insight and makes good use of it.

In discussing these two patients, I do not mean to emphasize psychopathology or the details of their psychotherapy. I consider both of them intelligent, talented, and very likable people, although they are so totally different on the dimension of thick or thin boundaries.

THE BOUNDARY QUESTIONNAIRE

Please try to rate each of the statements from 0 to 4. 0 indicates no, not at all, or not at all true of me. 4 indicates yes, definitely, or very true of me.

Please try to answer all of the questions and statements as quickly as you can.

1. When I awake in the morning, I am not sure whether I am really awake for a few minutes. 0 1 2 3 4

2. I have had unusual reactions to alcohol.
   0 1 2 3 4

3. My feelings blend into one another. 0 1 2 3 4

4. I am very close to my childhood feelings.
   0 1 2 3 4

5. I am very careful about what I say to people until I get to know them really well. 0 1 2 3 4

6. I am very sensitive to other people's feelings.
   0 1 2 3 4

7. I like to pigeonhole things as much as possible.
   0 1 2 3 4

8. I like solid music with a definite beat. 0 1 2 3 4

9. I think children have a special sense of joy and wonder that is later often lost. 0 1 2 3 4

10. In an organization, everyone should have a definite place and a specific role. 0 1 2 3 4

11. People of different nations are basically very much alike.
 0 1 2 3 4

12. There are a great many forces influencing us which science does not understand at all. 0 1 2 3 4

13. I have dreams, daydreams, nightmares in which my body or someone else's body is being stabbed, injured, or torn apart. 0 1 2 3 4

14. I have had unusual reactions to marijuana.
 0 1 2 3 4

15. Sometimes I don't know whether I am thinking or feeling.
 0 1 2 3 4

16. I can remember things from when I was less than three years old. 0 1 2 3 4

17. I expect other people to keep a certain distance.
 0 1 2 3 4

18. I think I would be a good psychotherapist.
 0 1 2 3 4

19. I keep my desk and worktable neat and well organized.
 0 1 2 3 4

20. I think it might be fun to wear medieval armor.
 0 1 2 3 4

21. A good teacher needs to help a child remain special.
 0 1 2 3 4

22. When making a decision, you shouldn't let your feelings get in the way. 0 1 2 3 4

23. Being dressed neatly and cleanly is very important. 0 1 2 3 4

24. There is a time for thinking and there is a time for feeling; they should be kept separate. 0 1 2 3 4

25. My daydreams don't always stay in control. 0 1 2 3 4

26. I have had unusual reactions to coffee or tea. 0 1 2 3 4

27. For me, things are black or white; there are no shades of gray. 0 1 2 3 4

28. I had a difficult and complicated childhood. 0 1 2 3 4

29. When I get involved with someone, I know exactly who I am and who the other person is. We may cooperate, but we maintain our separate selves. 0 1 2 3 4

30. I am easily hurt. 0 1 2 3 4

31. I get to appointments right on time. 0 1 2 3 4

32. I like heavy solid clothing. 0 1 2 3 4

33. Children and adults have a lot in common. They should give themselves a chance to be together without any strict roles. 0 1 2 3 4

34. In getting along with other people in an organization, it is very important to be flexible and adaptable.
0 1 2 3 4

35. I believe many of the world's problems could be solved if only people trusted each other more. 0 1 2 3 4

36. Either you are telling the truth or you are lying; that's all there is to it. 0 1 2 3 4

37. I spend a lot of time daydreaming, fantasizing, or in reverie. 0 1 2 3 4

38. I am afraid I may fall apart completely. 0 1 2 3 4

39. I like to have beautiful experiences without analyzing them or trying to understand them in detail.
0 1 2 3 4

40. I have definite plans for my future. I can lay out pretty well what I expect year by year at least for the next few years.
0 1 2 3 4

41. I can usually tell what another person is thinking or feeling without anyone saying anything. 0 1 2 3 4

42. I am unusually sensitive to loud noises and to bright lights. 0 1 2 3 4

43. I am good at keeping accounts and keeping track of my money. 0 1 2 3 4

44. I like stories that have a definite beginning, middle, and end. 0 1 2 3 4

45. I think an artist must in part remain a child.
0 1 2 3 4

46. A good organization is one in which all the lines of responsibility are precise and clearly established.
0 1 2 3 4

47. Each nation should be clear about its interests and its own boundaries, as well as the interests and boundaries of other nations. 0 1 2 3 4

48. There is a place for everything, and everything should be in its place. 0 1 2 3 4

49. Every time something frightening happens to me, I have nightmares or fantasies or flashbacks involving the frightening event. 0 1 2 3 4

50. I feel unsure of who I am at times. 0 1 2 3 4

51. At times I feel happy and sad all at once.
0 1 2 3 4

52. I have a clear memory of my past. I could tell you pretty well what happened year by year. 0 1 2 3 4

53. When I get involved with someone, we sometimes get too close. 0 1 2 3 4

54. I am a very sensitive person. 0 1 2 3 4

55. I like things to be spelled out precisely and specifically.
0 1 2 3 4

56. I think a good teacher must remain in part a child.
    0 1 2 3 4

57. I like paintings and drawings with clean outlines and no blurred edges. 0 1 2 3 4

58. A good relationship is one in which everything is clearly defined and spelled out. 0 1 2 3 4

59. People are totally different from each other.
    0 1 2 3 4

60. When I wake up, I wake up quickly and I am absolutely sure I am awake. 0 1 2 3 4

61. At times I have felt as if I were coming apart.
    0 1 2 3 4

62. My thoughts blend into one another. 0 1 2 3 4

63. I had a difficult and complicated adolescence.
    0 1 2 3 4

64. Sometimes it's scary when one gets too involved with another person. 0 1 2 3 4

65. I enjoy soaking up atmosphere even if I don't understand exactly what's going on. 0 1 2 3 4

67.* I like paintings or drawings with soft and blurred edges.
    0 1 2 3 4

*There is no item 66 on the Boundary Questionnaire; there is a total of 145 items on the questionnaire.

68. A good parent has to be a bit of a child too.
0 1 2 3 4

69. I cannot imagine marrying or living with someone of another religion. 0 1 2 3 4

70. It is very hard to empathize truly with another person because people are so different. 0 1 2 3 4

71. All important thought involves feelings, too.
0 1 2 3 4

72. I have dreams and daydreams or nightmares in which I see isolated body parts—arms, legs, heads, and so on.
0 1 2 3 4

73. Things around me seem to change their size and shape.
0 1 2 3 4

74. I can easily imagine myself to be an animal or what it might be like to be an animal. 0 1 2 3 4

75. I feel very separate and distinct from everyone else.
0 1 2 3 4

76. When I am in a new situation, I try to find out precisely what is going on and what the rules are as soon as possible. 0 1 2 3 4

77. I enjoy(ed) geometry; there are simple, straightforward rules, and everything fits. 0 1 2 3 4

78. A good parent must be able to empathize with his or her children, to be their friend and playmate at the same time.
0 1 2 3 4

79. I cannot imagine living with or marrying a person of another race. 0 1 2 3 4

80. People are so different that I never know what someone else is thinking or feeling. 0 1 2 3 4

81. Beauty is a very subjective thing. I know what I like, but I wouldn't expect anyone else to agree.
0 1 2 3 4

82. In my daydreams, people kind of merge into one another or one person turns into another. 0 1 2 3 4

83. My body sometimes seems to change its size or shape.
0 1 2 3 4

84. I get overinvolved in things. 0 1 2 3 4

85. When something happens to a friend of mine or a lover, it is almost as if it happened to me. 0 1 2 3 4

86. When I work on a project, I don't like to tie myself down to a definite outline. I rather like to let my mind wander.
0 1 2 3 4

87. Good solid frames are very important for a picture or a painting. 0 1 2 3 4

88. I think children need strict discipline. 0 1 2 3 4

89. People are happier with their own kind than when they mix. 0 1 2 3 4

90. East is East and West is West, and never the twain shall meet. (Kipling) 0 1 2 3 4

91. There are definite rules and standards, which one can learn, about what is and is not beautiful.
0 1 2 3 4

92. In my dreams, people sometimes merge into each other or become other people. 0 1 2 3 4

93. I believe I am influenced by forces which no one can understand. 0 1 2 3 4

94. When I read something, I get so involved that it can be difficult to get back to reality. 0 1 2 3 4

95. I trust people easily. 0 1 2 3 4

96. When I am working on a project, I make a careful detailed outline and then follow it closely.
0 1 2 3 4

97. The movies and TV shows I like the best are the ones where there are good guys and bad guys and you always know who they are. 0 1 2 3 4

98. If we open ourselves to the world, we find that things go better than expected. 0 1 2 3 4

99. Most people are sane; some people are crazy; there is no in-between. 0 1 2 3 4

100. I have had déjà vu experiences. 0 1 2 3 4

101. I have a very definite sense of space around me.
0 1 2 3 4

102. When I really get involved in a game or in playing at something, it's sometimes hard when the game stops and the rest of the world begins. 0 1 2 3 4

103. I am a very open person. 0 1 2 3 4

104. I think I would enjoy being an engineer.
0 1 2 3 4

105. There are no sharp dividing lines between normal people, people with problems, and people who are considered psychotic or crazy. 0 1 2 3 4

106. When I listen to music, I get so involved that it is sometimes difficult to get back to reality. 0 1 2 3 4

107. I am always at least a little bit on my guard.
0 1 2 3 4

108. I am a down-to-earth, no-nonsense kind of person.
0 1 2 3 4

109. I like houses with flexible spaces, where you can shift things around and make different uses of the same rooms. 0 1 2 3 4

110. Success is largely a matter of good organization and keeping good records. 0 1 2 3 4

111. Everyone is a little crazy at times. 0 1 2 3 4

112. I have daymares. 0 1 2 3 4

113. I awake from one dream into another.
0 1 2 3 4

114. Time slows down and speeds up for me. Time passes very differently on different occasions.
0 1 2 3 4

115. I feel at one with the world. 0 1 2 3 4

116. Sometimes I meet someone and trust him or her so completely that I can share just about everything about myself at the first meeting. 0 1 2 3 4

117. I think I would enjoy being the captain of a ship.
0 1 2 3 4

118. Good fences make good neighbors. 0 1 2 3 4

119. My dreams are so vivid that even later I can't tell them from waking reality. 0 1 2 3 4

120. I have often had the experience of different senses coming together. For example, I have felt that I could smell a color, or see a sound, or hear an odor.
0 1 2 3 4

121. I read things straight through from beginning to end. (I don't skip or go off on interesting tangents.)
0 1 2 3 4

122. I have friends and I have enemies, and I know which are which. 0 1 2 3 4

123. I think I would enjoy being some kind of a creative artist.
0 1 2 3 4

124. A man is a man and a woman is a woman; it is very important to maintain that distinction.
0 1 2 3 4

125. I know exactly what parts of town are safe and what parts are unsafe. 0 1 2 3 4

126. I have had the experience of not knowing whether I was imagining something or it was actually happening.
0 1 2 3 4

127. When I recall a conversation or a piece of music, I hear it just as though it were happening there again right in front of me. 0 1 2 3 4

128. I think I would enjoy a really loose, flexible job where I could write my own job description. 0 1 2 3 4

129. All men have something feminine in them and all women have something masculine in them. 0 1 2 3 4

130. In my dreams, I have been a person of the opposite sex.
0 1 2 3 4

131. I have had the experience of someone calling me or speaking my name and not being sure whether it was really happening or I was imagining it.
0 1 2 3 4

132. I can visualize something so vividly that it is just as though it is happening right in front of me.
0 1 2 3 4

133. I think I could be a good fortune-teller or a medium.
0 1 2 3 4

134. In my dreams, I am always myself. 0 1 2 3 4

135. I see auras or fields of energy around people.
0 1 2 3 4

136. I can easily imagine myself to be someone of the opposite sex. 0 1 2 3 4

137. I like clear, precise borders. 0 1 2 3 4

138. I have had the feeling that someone who is close to me was in danger or was hurt, although I had no ordinary way of knowing it, and later found out that it was true.
0 1 2 3 4

139. I have a very clear and distinct sense of time.
0 1 2 3 4

140. I like houses where rooms have definite walls and each room has a definite function. 0 1 2 3 4

141. I have had dreams that later came true.
0 1 2 3 4

142. I like fuzzy borders. 0 1 2 3 4

143. I have had "out of body" experiences during which my mind seems to leave, or actually has left, my body.
0 1 2 3 4

144. I like straight lines. 0 1 2 3 4

145. I like wavy or curved lines better than I like straight lines.
0 1 2 3 4

146. I feel sure that I can empathize with the very old.
    0 1 2 3 4

SCORING THE BOUNDARY QUESTIONNAIRE

All the questions listed in the left-hand column (labeled "Thick to thin") are "thin" items; the questions in the right-hand column (labeled "Thin to thick") are "thick" items. The difference should be clear from reading the items.

Under each number in the left-hand column, enter the score the subject has circled for that item. Under each number in the right-hand column, enter the *inverse* of the subject's score, according to the following table:

4=0
3=1
2=2
1=3
0=4

Add the scores entered in both columns to obtain the scores on each of the twelve categories and the overall score (SumBound). On the average, the total for all questions is 250–300.

Boundary Questionnaire Score Sheet

	Thick to Thin *0 4*	*Thin to Thick* *0 4*	*Score*
Category 1: Sleep/wake/dream	1 13 25 37 49 72 82 92 112 113 119 130	60 134	27
Category 2: Unusual experiences	2 14 26 38 50 61 73 83 93 100 114 120 126 131 135 138 141 143	(101, not included in the score.)	35
Category 3: Thoughts, feelings, moods	3 15 39 51 62 74 84 94 102 106 115 127 132 136	27 139	35
Category 4: Childhood, adolescence, adulthood	4 16 28 63	40 52	13
Category 5: Interpersonal	41 53 64 85 95 103 116 146	5 29 122 125 (17, 75, 107, not included in the score.)	31
Category 6: Sensitivity	6 18 30 42 54		18
Category 7: Neat, exact, precise	65 86	7 19 31 43 55 76 96 108 121	32
Category 8: Edges, lines, clothing	67 109 123 133 142 145 128	44 57 77 87 97 104 117 137 140 144 (8, 20, 32, not included in the score.)	56
Category 9: Opinions about children and others	9 21 33 45 56 68 78	88	29
Category 10: Opinions about organizations and relationships	34 98	10 22 46 58 69 79 89 110	29

Personal total 247

World Total 120

Sum bound 367

Boundary Questionnaire Score Sheet (*Continued*)

Thick to Thin 0 4	*Thin to Thick* 0 4	*Score*
Category 11: Opinions about peoples, nations, groups		
11 35 105 111 129	23 47 59 70 80 90 99 118 124	43
Category 12: Opinions about beauty, truth		
12 71 81	24 36 48 91	19
	Total score (SumBound)	___

Cat #1 1,1,3,4,1,2,4,3,1,2,0 4,/1,0,

Cat #2 1,4,0,4,3,3,0,0,4,4,3,0,0,2,3,0,4,0

Cat 3 4,2,4,4,4,3,3,0,0,1,2,1,2,1/4,0,

Cat 4 4,0,3,2/4,0,

Cat 5 3,2,1,4.4,4.2/3,3,4,1,

Cat 6 4,4,4,2,4/=

Cat 7 4 4/4,3,1,4,1,4,3,3,1,=

Cat 8 4,4,4,1,3,4/3,4,4,3,4,4,4,4,3,3

Cat 9 4,4,3,4,4,4,4/2

Cat 10 4,4,/3,3,1,3,4,3,4

Cat 11 3,4,4,4 4/0,1,4,4,3,4,4,3,1

Cat 12 4,4 0/2,4,1,4

WT 120+

CHAPTER 5

The Boundary Questionnaire in Relation to Other Personality Measures

THE BOUNDARY QUESTIONNAIRE was designed to quantify the concept of thick and thin boundaries. In the last chapter we have examined it in detail, have begun to see how it distinguished groups of people, and looked at the demographic and clinical characteristics of people who scored extremely thin or extremely thick.

The Boundary Questionnaire is a new measure, but is it really measuring something new, or does it merely duplicate what other measures are already doing? Some psychologists, for example, especially those who talk of "permeable boundaries" or "boundary defects," may think that "thin boundaries" is just another way of saying "sick" or "vulnerable to psychological illness." It should be clear by now that I do not share this view. In this section I examine this question and the broader question of how the Boundary Questionnaire relates to other personality measures. At present we have considerable data allowing us to relate the Boundary Questionnaire to the MMPI and limited data relating it to a number of other measures.

THE MMPI

The Minnesota Multiphasic Personality Inventory, usually called the MMPI, is the most widely used personality measure, at least in the United States and Canada. Since its introduction in 1943,* it has been taken by several million people. The MMPI consists of 566 statements to be marked either "true" or "false." It was originally designed to measure various types of psychopathology, and its most commonly used scales therefore have clinical names: hypochondriasis, depression, hysteria, psychopathic deviancy, masculinity-femininity, paranoia, psychasthenia, schizophrenia, hypomania, and social introversion; a large number of less frequently used clinical and nonclinical scales exist as well. Many of these terms are not in current use, so it would not make sense to discuss them in detail. The principal advantage of the MMPI is that so much is known about it, because it has been so widely used and examined in any number of specified groups, including normal populations. It must be kept in mind that someone who scores high on the paranoia (Pa) scale, for instance, is not thereby considered clinically paranoid. Such a score means only that the subject answered a group of the true-false items similarly

*A new version, called MMPI-2, has recently been introduced, but all studies up to 1989, including all studies mentioned here, used the standard MMPI.

to the way they were answered by groups of patients who were diagnosed as paranoid.

The MMPI also contains three other scales, sometimes known as reliability scales, called L, F, and K. L, sometimes called the Lie scale, measures a tendency to lie or at least to exaggerate in the direction of being too good or too perfect; it includes statements such as "I get angry sometimes" and "Once in a while I put off until tomorrow what I ought to do today." Marking these "false" increases one's L-score. The F scale measures the tendency to give infrequent responses, responses given by less than 5 percent of the normal population. A high F-scale score can be obtained by a person who does not understand the questions, is confused in some way, or answers at random, but with subjects who understand the questions and answer seriously, it can indicate having a lot of unusual experiences or opinions. Finally, the K scale measures defensiveness or not wanting to admit to problems.

Three hundred of the first 866 people who took the Boundary Questionnaire also took the MMPI, so we are in a good position to examine relationships between the two measures. Table 3 gives the correlations between the overall boundary measure SumBound (high scores equal thinness) and the MMPI scales in 299 persons.

Although many of the correlations are statistically significant, none are high enough so that we would say the MMPI scale is measuring the same thing as the Boundary Questionnaire. This fact may be important, because in our initial work with nightmare sufferers we suggested a relationship between nightmares and a vulnerability to schizophrenia. Because the nightmare sufferers do score

Table 3 Correlations of SumBound (Thinness of Boundaries) with MMPI Scales (K-corrected scales) in 299 Subjects

	L	*F*	*K*	*Hs*	*D*	*Hy*	*Pd*	*Mf(m)*	*Mf(f)*	*Pa*	*Pt*	*Sc*	*Ma*	*Si*
SumBound	−.31*	.32*	−.37*	−.08	.02	.02	.27*	.40*	.00	.41*	.21*	.25*	.30*	.07

*Significant at $p < .001$

very thin on the Boundary Questionnaire, and because the MMPI schizophrenia (Sc) scale can be seen as measuring not actual schizophrenia but perhaps a tendency towards schizophrenia, some researchers working with us expected an extremely high correlation between SumBound and Sc. Such a relationship was not found; in fact, several of the other MMPI scales showed a higher correlation with SumBound. Thus the Boundary Questionnaire is definitely not measuring the same thing as the MMPI Sc scale.

It is also of importance that the overall boundary score SumBound showed significant correlations with some but not all of the clinical MMPI scales. There was absolutely no relationship with the three scales sometimes lumped together as "neurotic" scales: hypochondriasis, depression, and hysteria, the scales most often elevated in people who have a variety of anxiety disorders and depressive disorders. Nor was there any relationship with the social introversion scale. It is clear, therefore, that the Boundary Questionnaire is not a general measure of sickness or psychopathology. People with thin boundaries appear to be no more "neurotic" or "introverted" than those with thick boundaries.

The scales with which SumBound did show significant correlations, however, form an interesting pattern. Having thin boundaries on the Boundary Questionnaire correlated best with high scores on paranoia (Pa), masculinity-femininity (Mf) in males, the F scale, and hypomania (Ma). And it correlated negatively with the L and K scales; people with thick boundaries tended to score higher on these two scales.

Do these relationships make sense? Do they show that

people with thin boundaries, though not "sick" overall, are after all paranoid or manic, while those with thick boundaries are defensive and liars? We cannot come to any such dramatic conclusion. Pa, the scale with the highest correlation to thin boundaries, is often considered a measure of sensitivity, especially interpersonal sensitivity, when tested in nonclinical populations. Here Pa refers to an awareness of others, to wondering what others are thinking, rather than being sure that others are against one. This sort of sensitivity was certainly found in interviews with the nightmare sufferers and others with thin boundaries, and in fact questions relating to sensitivity are one of the twelve subject-matter categories making up the Boundary Questionnaire.

High Mf scores are found in men who are willing to accept things in themselves that are sometimes considered feminine, such as a willingness to cry or an interest in flowers or fashion. In the discussion of types of boundaries in chapter 2, I suggested that this was one type of boundary, related to sexual identity. Therefore it is not surprising to find that overall thinness of boundaries has a positive relationship to Mf in males, which represents loosening or thinning of one type of boundary.

In this regard, it is of interest that the average man taking the MMPI in the 1980s or 1990s scores considerably "above average" on the Mf scale. The MMPI averages were based on men taking the test in the 1940s, and the entire male population has shifted somewhat in the direction of allowing or admitting to more "femininity." Thus men in general can now be considered thinner on this particular type of boundary, in comparison with men in the 1940s. (Interpretation of Mf in women is less clear;

in any case it shows no relationship to the Boundary Questionnaire, so it will not be discussed here.)

The relationship between SumBound and the F scale (infrequency scale) is also of interest. In our sample, I was personally acquainted with many of the subjects, and there is no question that they understood the MMPI questions and took the test in a serious fashion. For those who had a high F, this is an indication that they really did have unusual experiences, and opinions, and apparently that was more true of those with thin boundaries. This conclusion is hardly surprising when we consider that among the items included in the F scale are "I have a nightmare every few nights" and "Most any time I would rather sit and daydream than do anything else," which we would certainly expect to be affirmed more often by people with thin boundaries.

The Ma (hypomania) scale refers to overactivity, excitement, and flight of ideas; apparently these characteristics are found more in people who score high (thin) on the Boundary Questionnaire. We had not specifically expected this relationship with boundaries, but it is consistent with my clinical experience with at least some patients with thin boundaries. Heather, the young woman musician described in the last chapter, fits the description of someone who scores high on the Ma scale, and indeed she did score high on Ma as well as very thin on the Boundary Questionnaire.

The two MMPI scales that showed significant negative correlations with boundary thinness are also of interest. The relationship with the K scale was one I had predicted, because K measures defensiveness, and as we have seen, several kinds of defenses are thick-boundary characteristics; people with thin boundaries, especially those with nightmares, were felt by interviewers to be "undefended." The correlation of SumBound with the K scale is consistent with the view that thick boundaries involve solid or heavy defenses of some kind.

We had not specifically predicted any relationship between SumBound and the L scale, which scores the "unbelievably good" items. In most situations L is not a very sensitive scale; not many people maintain that they like everyone they know or that they never put off until tomorrow what they could do today. We did, however, find a relationship: those who answered in this way were more likely to score thick on the Boundary Questionnaire. This correlation can perhaps best be explained if one considers that the L scale also represents a kind of defense, a denial that one could be imperfect. As we saw in chapter 4, those who scored very thick tended to be perfectionistic.

Overall it appears that the Boundary Questionnaire is not measuring the same thing as the MMPI or any one of the scales of the MMPI. And there is no correlation whatever between the Boundary Questionnaire and the neurotic scales or the introversion scale of the MMPI. The pattern of correlations, however, suggests that several of the clinical MMPI scales are measuring some things that can be seen as part of thin boundaries such as sensitivity and, in males, the willingness to acknowledge one's feminine aspects. The correlations also show, even more than we had expected, that the measures of defensiveness (K scale) and even denial of any imperfection (L scale) are related to thick boundaries. For more detail see Appendix, table A-2.

RORSCHACH MEASURES

Among the other personality measures that might be related to the Boundary Questionnaire are the Rorschach measures we have already referred to in chapter 3, especially those that measure barrier, penetration, and boundary deficit. Since the Rorschach test involves a great deal of time and special expertise, data are available on only relatively small groups who have taken both the Boundary Questionnaire and the Rorschach.

Ross Levin (1986) obtained Rorschach measures as well as the Boundary Questionnaire in sixty students, thirty with frequent nightmares and thirty with few or no nightmares. The Rorschachs were scored for Blatt and Ritzler's measures of boundary deficit—responses involving "contamination," "fabulized combinations," and "confabulation" (1974)—and also for Fisher and Cleveland's (1968) measures of "barrier" and "penetration." The principal finding of the study was that the nightmare group had much thinner boundaries on the Boundary Questionnaire and higher scores for Blatt's boundary deficit measure, when compared with the no-nightmare group. The two groups did not differ, however, on barrier and penetration scores. Across the sixty subjects, SumBound (thinness on the Boundary Questionnaire) showed modest positive correlations (r between .20 and .30, $p < .05$) with Blatt's measure as well as with penetration, but no correlation with barrier.

Holiday Adair, working with us in Boston, studied thirty-two patients at a mental health center who had taken the Rorschach as well as the Boundary Questionnaire. In this group she found no significant correlation between SumBound and either barrier or penetration on the Rorschach, nor was there any correlation between the major factors of the Boundary Questionnaire and either barrier or penetration. There was a similar lack of correlation with barrier and penetration in a group of thirty-eight evening-school students (Adair 1990).

On the basis of the data available so far, therefore, it appears that the measure of barrier on the Rorschach is definitely not measuring the same thing as the Boundary Questionnaire. This finding is somewhat surprising, in view of the fact that the barrier measure was designed to relate to the body boundary—the skin. Yet perhaps it is not too surprising in that barrier appears to relate to an immediate perceptual awareness of one's skin; as we saw in chapter 3, the barrier score is affected by skin disease, by exercise, and by rubbing the skin (Fisher 1986). Thus it is perhaps less related to enduring personality traits. And only one of three studies showed a correlation between thin boundaries and penetration. There is, however, some support for a relationship between thin boundaries on the Boundary Questionnaire and boundary deficit (Blatt's measures) on the Rorschach, but it is based on only one study so far.

MEASURES OF HYPNOTIZABILITY

In view of what we have said about thin boundaries in the senses of merging, lack of defensiveness, letting other people in, and having vivid imagery sometimes indistinguishable from reality, it seems likely that there would be some relationship between boundary scores and measures of hypnotizability. Indeed, in a group of two hundred students, Deirdre Barrett (1989) demonstrated highly significant correlations between total boundary scores (SumBound) and three different scales measuring aspects of hypnotizability: the Harvard Group Scale of Hypnotic Susceptibility, Tellegen's Absorption Scale, and the Field inventory. The highest correlation ($r = .54, p < .001$) was with the Absorption Scale, a pencil-and-paper test dealing with spontaneous hypnosis-like experiences (Tellegen and Atkinson 1974). This finding confirms our impression that people with thin boundaries tend on the average to be more suggestible or hypnotizable than those with thick boundaries.

OTHER MEASURES

Only small amounts of data are available linking the Boundary Questionnaire directly with other measures of personality. In the study by Levin (1986) on students with and without nightmares, two different measures of "schizotypal personality" were also obtained. These were the Schizotypy Questionnaire (Chapman, Chapman, and Raulin 1978) and the Schedule for Schizotypal Personalities, based on a psychiatric interview (Baron, Agnis, and Gruen 1981). In addition to the finding that the students with frequent nightmares scored higher on these measures of schizotypy, Levin found significant positive correlations between thin boundaries and both measures of schizotypy. These correlations are consistent with our finding that some of the original subjects with frequent nightmares, described in chapter 1, as well as those who scored extremely thin on the Boundary Questionnaire, were given the diagnosis of schizotypal personality disorder.

One study performed by Andrea Celenza (1986) examined boundary characteristics of patients with the diagnosis of either borderline personality disorder or narcissistic personality disorder. In small groups of patients, she confirmed her hypothesis that those with borderline personality disorder scored thin on the Boundary Questionnaire. Results with the other group were less clear. She also reported significant correlations in the expected direction between thickness on the Boundary Questionnaire and a measure called Maintenance of Emotional Separation (Corcoran 1983) as well as a measure called Narcissistic-Borderline Defense against Affects Scale (Modell 1975). These results suggest that, not unexpectedly, scoring thick on the Boundary Questionnaire is related to maintaining emotional distance from others and defending oneself against strong emotion.

So far, there is not much more data linking the Boundary Questionnaire directly with other personality measures. (Some relationships with measures connected to sleep and dreaming and to mental and physical illness will be discussed in later chapters.) It would be very useful to examine correlations with some of the other widely used personality measures such as Eysenck's measures of introversion/extroversion, neuroticism, and psychoticism (1967, 1976) or the personality "superfactors" first developed by Norman (1963) and given many different names. My colleagues and I have examined the content of these other personality measures, and our impression is that the Boundary Questionnaire will not turn out to be closely related to any of them. On the Eysenck measures any relationship between the Boundary Questionnaire and introversion-extroversion or neuroticism is very unlikely, although on the basis of the MMPI results, we expect we may find some degree of relationship to psychoticism.

The data relating the Boundary Questionnaire with other established measures are limited, but they do indicate that thin and thick boundaries are unrelated to neuroticism or introversion, as measured on the MMPI. Thinness on the Boundary Questionnaire does appear to be related to quite a range of other measures, however, such as hypnotizability and absorption, schizotypy, sensitivity, a tendency not to maintain emotional separation or defenses, and, as will be seen in chapter 9, the ability to recall dreams. All these relationships are in the direction expected from our description of the types of boundaries in chapter 2.

PART TWO

BOUNDARIES IN OUR LIVES

Chapter 6

The Origin and Development of Boundaries

How do our boundary structures develop? Are people who have especially thick or especially thin boundaries born with them, or does something happen during childhood or adolescence to make them that way? And once our boundaries are formed, do they stay the same throughout our lives, or do they change with age? What effects do stress and trauma have on our boundary structures?

Looking at this daunting set of questions, I could be a good scientist and give one simple, entirely truthful answer: I don't know. The data are clearly not available to support any definite conclusions. Nonetheless, it is permissible and perhaps useful to speculate and form hypotheses on the basis of very limited data; almost all psychoanalytic and other clinical work begins with hypotheses based on a few cases. In this chapter I will venture a few hypotheses about the questions just posed.

NATURE, NURTURE, OR BOTH?

Is there an inborn tendency to develop a particular structure of thick or thin boundaries? And whether or not there are genetic factors, does environment make a difference? If so, are these environmental factors prenatal biological factors, birth-related events, events in infancy or early childhood, or perhaps interpersonal or other aspects of the environment that continue to affect us and mold our boundaries as we grow up?

On the basis of bits of clinical evidence, I believe that genetic factors do play a role. In a number of patients and subjects I have interviewed there appeared to be a family tendency; people who were thin or thick enough to recognize the pattern in themselves often identified a similar pattern in one or more close family members. The determinants of this sort of family pattern could of course be environmental just as well as genetic, but in five cases of people who themselves had extremely thin boundaries I heard something like this:

> Yes, I've always been very open and sensitive, easily hurt, trusting; everything gets to me. I've been that way my whole life. And do you want to know something interesting about my family? My younger brother is exactly the same way, and so is my mother. But my sister and my father are just the opposite. Wow, you wouldn't believe how different they are. They're like stone walls!

This is exactly the pattern one would expect in families if the tendency to have thin or thick boundaries involved a simple genetic factor, perhaps even a single gene.

Of course, the evidence is extremely limited. Moreover, people are often highly inaccurate in describing their childhoods, especially when they are discussing emotional issues or when they have axes to grind. Before one could come to a definite conclusion, it would be important to study large families in which a pattern of thin or thick boundaries could be established, if possible through several generations. Twin studies would also be useful. My impression from reading numerous case studies in which identical twins, separated from birth or early childhood, were tested as adults (see for instance Shields 1962; Farber 1981) is that boundary structures in these twins were very similar. Obviously however, this issue would have to be studied directly, via the Boundary Questionnaire.

In addition to genetic factors, I believe that environmental factors must also be involved in the development of thick and thin boundaries. There is of course a huge clinical literature in child psychiatry and psychology concerning the gradual development of independence, autonomy, and identity (see for instance Noshpitz 1979). The development of these attributes, in which maturational as well as environmental factors play a role, can be thought of as part of the development of boundaries in childhood. The emphasis in child development, often studied from the point of view of presence or lack or pathology, is the necessary development of autonomy in the normal child. Poor development is sometimes conceptualized in terms of "lack of boundaries" or "boundary deficits." My interest here is a bit different: within the broad range of normal development, what determines who develops especially thick boundaries and who develops thin ones? Or can thin boundaries perhaps be understood as the lack of development, or the very delayed development, of thick boundaries?

One factor leading to thick boundaries, in the patients and research subjects I have seen, appears to be a strong identification, generally with a parent of the same sex. For example, Charles, the man with thick boundaries described in chapter 4, has an extremely solid identification with his father. He not only admires his father and emulates him consciously in some ways but also imitates him in ways Charles is not always conscious of, so that friends and relatives sometimes point out mannerisms or turns of phrase that are "just like his father," even though he is usually unaware of it. He was also brought up in a very traditional household, where the expectation that he follow in the footsteps of his father and other male relatives was strong.

Competition with siblings, especially older siblings of the same sex, may play a role as well. Three patients I saw in therapy, two men and one woman who scored extremely thick on the Boundary Questionnaire, all had older same-sex siblings about whom they experienced powerful competitive feelings. Of course, such competitive feelings are extremely common in younger siblings. But what struck me as out of the ordinary, much more powerful than average in these three persons, was their intense need to grow up fast, to become as adult as, or even more adult than, the brother or sister who had the advantage of being two to three years older.

Many younger siblings have this desire to catch up, but usually it is more or less in balance with an opposite tendency to enjoy the prerogatives of being younger: being taken care of, being babied and spoiled, not being the one who is blamed in conflicts with the older sibling, and so on. In these three cases of people who developed very thick boundaries, the first tendency—competition and growing up fast—was totally dominant. The second seemed almost totally absent; little wish to be babied or cared for emerged, even in long-term psychotherapy.

Finally, a very strong set of rules, a strong superego, was characteristic of the development of these three cases. The rules were internalized very early. In reporting their childhoods, none of the three could think of any pattern of rebellion against the rules. At most they reported an isolated instance of having broken a rule and being punished for it. Moreover, the feeling was that the rules had been right, they had been wrong, they had been punished, and that was it.

These are my only strong impressions so far as to factors related to the development of thick boundaries. Of course, these are not necessarily external factors impinging on the child but may themselves be influenced by the internally determined lines of development and maturation in the child. Being a younger sibling with an older sibling of the same sex may be an external factor, an independent variable, but the rest is less clear. Was the sibling unusually harsh or hard to deal with in some way, so that the young child had to grow up fast? Or would this younger sibling have reacted the same way to any older sibling? Was the father such an ideal model or such a powerful character that identification was imposed on his young son no matter what the son's predisposition? Or would the son's internal need for (and therefore tendency toward) identification produce the same result no matter what his father was actually like? Of course we do not know for sure; my impression in the cases I have seen is that there is some influence from both sides.

In a sense I am rehashing some old arguments in the field of child development regarding the roles played by internal maturational factors as opposed to external environmental factors in the development of the child in general as well as the development of specific features or conditions. In this case I am addressing myself to a new topic—the development of thick boundaries. But as I consider the clinical characteristics of people with very thick boundaries, it is clear to me that there is some overlap with the condition called obsessive-compulsive personality, or more broadly the character traits sometimes called obsessive-compulsive character or style.

In his classic book *Neurotic Styles* (1965), David Shapiro describes under the rubric of "obsessive-compulsive style," a sometimes exaggerated picture of some of the characteristics of people with thick boundaries: the sense of rules and regulations, the rigidity, the need to fit a definite role, the emphasis on "I should." There is a difference, however, in that some of his patients with these traits, and certainly patients diagnosed as obsessive-compulsive personality disorder, have a disorder in the sense that the personality traits are disturbing, usually to the patients themselves as well as to others. This is not generally the case with thick boundaries; having thick boundaries includes the most ego-syntonic parts of the obsessive-compulsive style (aspects viewed as acceptable parts of one's self). The people with thick boundaries I have described invariably *like* most aspects of their personalities. Having thick boundaries feels to them solid, reliable, autonomous, and independent; it is obviously the way to be. They usually consider someone with thin boundaries to be a bit "flaky." Nonetheless at least some of what has been written about the development of obsessive-compulsive character by Freud (1909), Anna Freud (1948), Wilhelm Reich (1933), Elizabeth Zetzel (1970), and others may be relevant to the development of thick boundaries.

Childhood antecedents leading to very thin boundaries in adulthood may include, first, an absence of the factors discussed above. There may be no strong identification with the same-sex parent, no older sibling of the same sex or no powerful need to catch up to the sibling, and no strong rules or strong introjected superego. The patients I have treated who have extremely thin boundaries—I am thinking especially of Heather and two other women—do have a definite lack of identification with their mothers; at most they have a very spotty, off-and-on identification. In each case the mother was either depressed or somehow ineffectual during the patient's childhood years.

Sometimes the childhood situation is more serious or traumatic. Laura, a woman who has shown considerable evidence of thin boundaries although she has not taken the Boundary Questionnaire, has serious problems with interpersonal relationships that pervaded her adolescence and have continued in her adult life. She also has rapid mood swings and is experiencing great difficulty in establishing her sense of identity. She was raped at age fifteen by a man several years older than she. She did not report the rape, and a few months later she started a long-term (though sporadic) sexual relationship with the man who had raped her! Much of her personal life, including her psychotherapy with two women therapists, revolved around her lack of interpersonal boundaries. She turned her first therapist into a friend and then discontinued therapy because it felt too close. She made progress in her second therapy, defending her fragile but developing boundaries with all her might; in an argument with a new boyfriend, when he seemed about to slap her, she said, "If you touch me, one of us will end up in the hospital!" Interestingly, she made almost the same comment to her mother when the two were having an argument.

In her childhood Laura had at times been neglected and at other times verbally and physically abused by her alcoholic mother. At still other times the mother had broken down and expected her daughter to care for her totally, even when Laura was only five to ten years old. At these times the daughter had been expected to mother her mother! And unfortunately this problematic mother was her only parent; her father had disappeared when Laura was quite young. In Laura's case it seems plausible that the constant boundary violations by her mother, and finally the rape at age fifteen, played major roles in producing her painfully thin interpersonal boundaries.

Laura's case is extreme, but there is increasing evidence that patients with the diagnosis of borderline personality disorder have experienced serious trauma in childhood (Herman et al. 1989), and patients with this diagnosis tend to score thin on the Boundary Questionnaire. Thus it is possible that childhood trauma can be one environmental factor responsible for thin boundaries, even though we have been unable to identify such trauma in most persons who score thin on the Boundary Questionnaire. The more common picture seems to be a child who takes unusually hard the ordinary, expectable traumas of childhood such as the birth of a younger sibling, suggesting that in these cases thin boundaries may already have been present at the time of the event. My best guess at this point is that the development of very thin boundaries depends on a genetic predisposition, usually combined with environmental factors which may include a lack of solid figures for identification, especially the parent of the same sex, and in some cases childhood trauma.

The development of thick or thin boundaries may also relate to the timing and the intensity of some well-known developments in later childhood. Child psychologists and psychiatrists are well aware of a series of important changes that most children undergo between the approximate ages of five and ten. These are the elementary school years, during which children acquire a multitude of skills and learn to adapt and relate to peers and teachers. Freud called this the latency period, when the sexual drives are relatively less active, between the turmoil of the Oedipal period and the resurgence of sexual interests at puberty. Erik Erikson refers to this time as the phase of "industry" (1950). It is recognized that as children enter this phase they become more serious and organized and lose some of the imagination, vivid imagery, and spontaneous creativity they had at the age of three or four.

We can think of this more or less universal phase as a time of thickening of boundaries. In this phase children are expected to learn to concentrate, to focus their attention, to organize their time, and to follow through on assignments. They also develop a sense of group, of friends and enemies. A glance at the many types of boundaries discussed in chapter 2 and listed in table 1 will make it clear that many if not all of these boundaries become thicker or more solid between the ages of approximately five and ten.

Perhaps a major determinant of adult boundary structure lies in the timing and intensity of this thickening of boundaries during latency. An adult with thick boundaries may be one who has had a relatively early and intense strengthening of boundaries at this time (consistent with "growing up fast"). An adult with thin boundaries may have had a later-starting and less intense latency process and thus kept some of the thin-boundary characteristics of earlier childhood. In this sense thick means growing up fast and becoming adapted to the world rapidly, but it may also mean not growing any more, becoming a specialized creature, well adapted to a particular niche but less adaptable. Thin implies remaining a child to some extent, with more of the adaptability and creativity but also the vulnerability of the young child. (Biological factors that may underlie these differences are discussed in chapter 12.)

In summary I am suggesting that as young children we all have thin boundaries in many senses (though with individual differences), and the process of learning and adaptation at age five to ten inevitably involves the solidifying or thickening of boundaries. The rate and extent of this thickening, which probably has both genetic and environmental causes along the lines we have discussed, determines the eventual boundary structure of the adult.

DO BOUNDARIES CHANGE?

Once childhood is past, can changes still occur, or are we stuck with exactly the boundaries we formed in childhood? Among the adults, aged eighteen to seventy, who took the Boundary Questionnaire, age was negatively correlated with total boundary score ($r = -.32$); in other words older subjects tended to score thicker. Does this mean that we generally "thicken" as we grow older during our adult years? Possibly, but not necessarily. We did not test the same individuals over time, so the results could also indicate that people born before the 1960s have thicker boundaries than people born in the 1960s and early 1970s (when most of the undergraduate students in our sample were born) and that both groups may more or less maintain their individual boundary styles for the rest of their lives.

This second possibility may be plausible; in the United States and much of the Western world, the late 1960s was a period when certain thin-boundary characteristics were valued more highly than they usually are. It is possible that young children growing up at that time may somehow have absorbed these values. We cannot know for sure unless we test the same people on the Boundary Questionnaire over a period of decades.

Nonetheless my impression, based on observations of patients and friends over many years, is that although we maintain much of our basic boundary structure, changes do occur and boundaries tend to thicken with age. There is a bit less spontaneous imagery and imagination, and certain kinds of creativity tend to decline. We are less inclined to form new relationships, and we are also less vulnerable. For most people, the skin toughens a little as we get older; it is somewhat more difficult to be open to new experiences, to be flexible, to adopt a whole new way of looking at things. But of course there are many exceptions. Boundaries can remain thin or even get thinner with age, especially in people who were somewhat rigid or obsessional and who have been successful, with or without the help of psychotherapy, in loosening up. Those who continue to grow and broaden as they get older can be thought of as developing thinner boundaries, at least in some senses. And of course there are mixtures; in some people, different boundaries may change in different directions.

Aside from the general tendencies related to age, it is possible for our boundaries to change in a number of ways. Again, the Boundary Questionnaire is too new to have allowed for long-term studies, and it may not even be the best way to measure such changes, because some of its questions are directed at long-term tendencies or personality traits. Insofar as I can judge boundary structure on the basis of interviews, psychotherapy sessions, and limited data from the Boundary Questionnaire, I would say that boundaries can certainly change in both directions, becoming thinner or thicker.

Sometimes the change can be a positive one. People with very thick boundaries may gradually learn to appreciate things outside their usual "walls," either through psychotherapy or simply in the course of life. The old saying that "travel broadens" is relevant here, applying not only to geographical travel but to travel in many senses. A person who starts out with the thick-boundary view that "My group (or my way) is right; the others are wrong. Period" and who spends time with the other group, or trying the other way, will often come out with a more flexible attitude and thinner boundaries in at least some senses. For example, I have known people who started with a thick-boundary attitude that shows up on one item of the Boundary Questionnaire—"Some people are sane; some people are crazy; there is no in-between"—and then worked at a mental health center for a time and drastically changed this particular piece of their boundaries.

Such a change is not very different from actually traveling to another country or culture and noticing that people there are basically not so different from the people one knows at home. This sort of change can be considered a very superficial kind of thinning, not a real personality change, yet often it is just what people with extremely thick boundaries need. They still maintain their inner thickness, their personal solidity, but they broaden their outlook and become less definite or authoritarian in their views about the world. Being very solid inside and yet broadminded about the world may in fact represent one sort of ideal. And sometimes the change goes further or deeper, and a person's friends will say "He's just not the same person since he worked there" or "It's amazing how she's mellowed."

Clinically my experience is that often a person with very thick boundaries may be terrified by the idea of thinning, of becoming looser, more open, or more feeling. I asked one such man to picture what would happen if he gave up some of the rigidity and some of the careful organized quality we had been discussing. Although he claimed he was no good at imagining things, a picture did come into his mind: he saw himself dissolving into a puddle in the street. It reminded him of a "giggly female" he knew who sometimes "just dissolved." He worried that he would dissolve in feeling, lose all sense of direction, and be unable to think, to plan, to accomplish things. He would lose all sense of himself and melt into one big puddle.

This frightening image was very significant to him, and it became important in our therapeutic work; in effect his image was of totally thin personal boundaries in all the most disturbing senses. This image may also be important theoretically in that it lends some clinical support to the legitimacy of our admittedly oversimplified approach of considering boundaries on a single broad continuum from thin to thick. When faced with possibly giving up or altering a few of his specific thick boundaries, this man's image was a total loss of all boundaries, all solidity as he turned into a puddle in the street.

In the other direction, a person with very thin boundaries may be able to thicken certain useful boundaries. I have seen a number of men and women with very thin boundaries, including Heather, introduced in chapter 4, who have learned, through bitter experience or psychotherapy or both, that they could not afford to be quite as automatically open and trusting as they had been in the past. They want and need some thickening, especially in interpersonal boundaries. These people slowly develop a thicker interpersonal boundary, which at first may feel external or uncomfortable but is extremely useful to them and can sometimes literally save their lives. They may still fall in love or feel they can trust someone at once, but nonetheless they learn to be cautious, to take some time, not to get involved too quickly. They insert a new boundary—a cautiousness or a delay—on the basis of their experience, or sometimes on the basis of insight and learning without the need for an actual traumatic experience.

THE EFFECTS OF STRESS AND TRAUMA

In the cases just described, the thinning or thickening of boundaries was definitely beneficial. Unfortunately that is not always the case; boundaries can also change in less wholesome ways. I have not seen anyone with thick boundaries turn into a puddle in the street, as my patient feared could happen, but a severe trauma followed by post-traumatic stress disorder represents a kind of tearing of boundaries. Certain boundaries suddenly become thin, often in maladaptive ways.

My colleagues and I have interviewed and treated a number of Vietnam War veterans who were having severe nightmares as part of a post-traumatic stress disorder (van der Kolk et al. 1984). These were young men who, as far as we could tell, had been fairly normal children and adolescents; they did not have the sensitivities, artistic tendencies, and other characteristics of the lifelong nightmare subjects, and in fact they reported having few or no nightmares until the age of seventeen or eighteen. At that time—at the surprisingly early age of seventeen and a half, on average—each had a horrible experience; in most cases, the young man's closest buddy was killed or badly wounded right next to him. From then on, or sometimes beginning a few months later, these young men suffered symptoms including not only nightmares but flashbacks and actute anxiety states, often with the theme of "him or me" or "how come he's dead and I'm alive?" (survivor guilt). The boundary separating them from their buddies, or from other people, had apparently been torn. One of them had a repetitive nightmare in which he was opening body bags and identifying the dead soldiers inside. He would open the last body bag, recognize himself inside it, and wake up screaming.

In these cases, any incident associated with the war, or with the buddy, or anything at all involving a strong emotion, could trigger a flashback or other reaction. These veterans had become vulnerable in a number of ways. They were sensitive—things "got to them"—in a way they had not been before. Obviously these young men, who apparently had had ordinary boundaries in childhood, had developed thin boundaries in at least certain specific areas in early adulthood.

Boundaries can also become thicker in relatively uncomfortable and maladaptive ways. I remember Percy, a young man with frequent nightmares. He was a painter who appeared to have considerable talent and had had prestigious exhibits of his paintings when he was only nineteen years old. He had all the characteristics of thin boundaries in childhood, had gone through a painful adolescence, but had remained extremely open, trusting, and close to people. At the age of nineteen or twenty, however, when he was faced with living by himself, trying to earn a living by his painting or some other way, and trying to develop a relationship with a girlfriend, his sensitivity to criticism, his tendency to be hurt and vulnerable, became unbearable.

I could see Percy trying to develop some sort of thicker boundary as a protection, but in his case the process did not appear to be going smoothly. He developed a thick protective boundary consisting of anger and rebellion against authority—"No one understands me," "The goddam system can't tolerate a true artist"—which he carried to extremes. He distanced himself not only from "authority" but from his former friends as well, and from his girlfriend; in his view, they all were taking the part of authority or the system and were against him. In other words, he developed a paranoid system as a makeshift thick boundary, a heavy suit of armor that did not fit well but to him was preferable to his intolerable naked, unarmored state.

Percy's case may not be unusual. I believe that in many patients with paranoid defenses or other ill-fitting thick boundaries (armor) there is or was a vulnerable artist inside. This young man represents one type of mixed boundaries: very thin boundaries inside, but a thick boundary on the outside. In chapter 10, we will discuss further various mixtures of boundaries.

I would suggest, on the basis of a great deal of clinical experience but no controlled studies as yet, that in general stressful conditions tend to produce thickening of boundaries in a number of senses. Often this is seen as defensiveness, defending oneself against a stressful environment, a tough world. On the other hand, I believe that stress serious enough to be called trauma can tear boundaries and make boundaries thinner, as we have seen. Of course, there can then be further developments. Victims of post-traumatic stress disorder, for instance, finding themselves thin and vulnerable in some ways and living in a tough world, may develop some thicker boundaries as a defense. They may become loners, avoiding all relationships because the emotion could trigger their terrifying flashbacks, or they may become gruff and angry, pushing people away. In these situations, boundary structure has clearly changed, in complicated ways; one gets the sense of a vulnerable area kept separate, heavily walled off from the rest of the person.

I have spoken so far of trauma in adolescence or young adulthood, when most boundaries are already formed. What about trauma in childhood, which would tear boundaries even as they are being formed? We know that serious childhood trauma—by no means a rare event, unfortunately—has the potential to produce a great deal of complex psychopathology. As we have seen, patients with the diagnosis of borderline personality disorder often have experienced sexual or physical abuse in childhood. They show evidence of thin or torn boundaries such as an inability to control emotions, an inability to keep out stimuli, a tendency to enter relationships quickly, or an intolerance for being alone. But they also attempt to form thick defensive boundaries, such as projection or a tendency to paranoia, and "splitting"—insisting on seeing others as totally good or totally evil. Their situation can be seen as somewhat similar to that of patients with post-traumatic stress disorder, but with more widespread thin, torn boundaries and usually less solid rigid, thick ones.

A more unusual and more dramatic result of especially severe childhood trauma is multiple personality disorder, in which two or more separate and independent personalities coexist in the same person. Multiple personality disorder can be seen as an even more extreme mixture of thin and thick boundaries than the conditions just discussed. Here boundaries are torn early and horribly by severe abuse. In barely formed boundaries, the tear is perhaps more complete, and as a reaction a more complete firming up or defensive thickening of certain boundaries produces walled-off or encapsulated total personalities. The vulnerable thin-boundary child is kept well hidden within one of the personalities, protected by thick walls; the other, later-formed personalities often function in great part as protection or defense.

CHAPTER 7

Ourselves and Others

FROM WHAT HAS BEEN SAID SO far about boundaries, it will be clear that our relationships with other people are heavily dependent on whether our boundaries are thick or thin. In this chapter, I will look at how the nature of our boundaries affects specific types of relationships with the outer world: close sexual and nonsexual relationships, group membership, and career choice. First, however, it will be instructive to look at the differences between men and women in their overall scores on the Boundary Questionnaire and their attitudes toward boundaries and relationships.

GENDER DIFFERENCES IN BOUNDARIES

All items in the Boundary Questionnaire were worded as carefully as possible to avoid any sexual bias; there were no questions that obviously would be answered differently by men and women. Nonetheless the results demonstrated clear-cut differences between men and women in boundary scores. Overall, women scored significantly thinner than men—thinner by about twenty points, or 8 percent of the overall score.

Examination of the category scores and the factor scores reveals that the difference is found in most but not all senses of boundary. Women scored significantly thinner than men on most of the twelve original content categories making up the Boundary Questionnaire. The differences were especially pronounced on the first eight categories constituting the Personal Total, describing personal experiences, feelings, sensitivities, and preferences. Women scored only slightly (nonsignificantly) thinner on the four categories constituting the World Total, describing opinions about the world. Women also scored somewhat thinner on almost all the factors of the Boundary Questionnaire, significantly thinner on six of them. On one factor, however—factor VIII, "belief in impenetrable intergroup boundaries"—women scored significantly thicker. This factor includes questions such as "I could never imagine marrying someone of another religion," "I could never imagine marrying someone of another race," and "East is East and West is West, and never the twain shall meet"(Appendix, table A-3).

The simple difference in boundary scores may not be as important as the way boundaries enter into men's and women's lives and the way they are experienced or valued. Judith Bevis, a member of our boundary research group in Boston, conducted an interesting study (1986) on groups of evening students at an urban university.

She demonstrated that the women in this group (most of them aged twenty-five to thirty) did have significantly thinner boundaries than the men on the Boundary Questionnaire. She then went on to relate boundary scores to a number of other measures in these same people, including measures of affective and interpersonal connectedness from the Rorschach test and measures of affiliation and isolation from the Thematic Apperception Test (TAT). Her most prominent finding was that the women tended to value certain aspects of thin boundaries, such as interpersonal connectedness, and to feel comfortable with them, whereas they found certain aspects of thick boundaries, such as autonomy, to be uncomfortable. The men in the sample tended toward the opposite viewpoints, considering autonomy and self-sufficiency as comfortable but merging or connectedness as less comfortable or desirable.

These results are not surprising; in fact, they are very consistent with an emerging body of literature on differences between men and women suggesting that women value connectedness and relationship more than do men. (See, for example, Gilligan 1982; Miller 1986). Carol Gilligan demonstrates dramatically that in making moral decisions women value maintaining connections with others and not hurting others relatively more than men do. Men base their moral decisions more on general principles. Jean Baher Miller states, "Women's sense of self becomes very much organized around being able to maintain affiliations and relationships. Eventually for many women the threat of disruption of connection is perceived not just as loss of a relationship but as something closer to a total loss of self."

RELATIONSHIPS

How one human being relates to another is an endless source of fascination. Just about every story ever written is about relationships or lack of relationships in one way or another. Great mysteries are involved. Why are we so attracted to A and not to B? How can we love someone whose individual qualities we don't especially like? Usually such questions cannot be answered by logical thought; our oldest, least understood urges and feelings are at play. Transference is everywhere, which simply means that our current loves and hates and friendships are inevitably influenced by the important relationships in our past.

Obviously boundaries are involved in relationships; for some people, this is in fact the primary and most obvious meaning of boundary. Do you "maintain your distance," "keep others out," or do you "get involved," "merge," "lose yourself in a relationship"? Thick boundaries in relationships could mean being completely self-sufficient, separate, a hermit. More often people with very thick boundaries live normal enough lives, but they are surrounded by a series of walls or defenses against what they perceive as excessive closeness. Andrew, whom we met in chapter 1, was extreme in this sense; he hardly spoke of relationships with other people at all, even in psychotherapy. When asked, he would say, "Oh, yes, my girlfriend and I get along fine. . . . Sure, sex is okay. . . . My mother? A wonderful woman, wonderful." Relationships existed, but they seemed somehow unimportant to him; he was not involved or was avoiding involvement. He did finally admit, "Well, there was one death that really got to me, but I can't talk about that." One gets a sense of walls, and in part the walls serve as defenses.

A person with extremely thin boundaries becomes overinvolved, so that at times it is unclear whether there are two people there, or just one. Heather, for example, truly could not imagine giving up her boyfriend because he was "part of her." This was not a figure of speech for her, but a deep feeling. Another woman said, "Growing older is terrible for me. I feel so young, but my skin is growing into my mother's skin with all its wrinkles. I can see my mother's body around me so clearly, and I'm growing into it."

Although the thin-boundary position often has a vulnerable or defenseless sense to it, it can also sometimes serve defensive purposes. Merging with someone, or for that matter losing oneself in romantic fantasy, can serve as a defense insofar as it keeps one from dealing with the hard realities of a relationship.

Neither extremely thick nor extremely thin boundaries in this sense seem very desirable for most of us. We think of a healthy relationship as made up of two individuals who have a reasonably firm sense of themselves so that they can comfortably relate, enjoy the other person, and become involved without losing their own identities. Yet it is interesting that we sometimes choose as ideals the impossibly thick or thin extremes. We have already noted Kipling's description of an ideal man in his poem "If." He includes the lines "If neither foes nor loving friends can hurt you, / If all men count with you, but none too much." Lately those lines have disturbed me. Would I really want to be a person whom neither foes nor friends could hurt? Isn't the thick-boundary position being taken to extremes? Yet our fiction, especially heroic stories for boys, is full of tough, independent, unhurtable (male) heroes. Perhaps we feel, or felt, that this idealization is necessary, at least at certain stages of our growing up, to help us fight the cold cruel world and conquer it. The rewards are great: if you can fulfill the conditions of the four verses, "Yours is the earth and everything that's in it, And—which is more—you'll be a man, my son."

The other extreme—the complete surrender of one's individuality in a total merging with the other—is also idealized in literature. Many great love stories end this way, and usually the lovers die in the process, for it would be impossible for the ideal to continue into everyday life. In great religious poetry, especially in the mystical traditions, the ideal is a giving up of oneself in a total merging with God. This ideal, too, occurs as an ultimate achievement, an ending. One who has achieved it does not return to argue with neighbors about property lines or join a computer dating service.

What happens in ordinary life? What sort of relationships do actual, nonideal people with thick or thin boundaries have? Among the patients and research subjects I interviewed and those who took the Boundary Questionnaire, everyone had human relationships of some kind, but a great many differences emerged. One striking fact was that the twenty people who scored thickest on the Boundary Questionnaire (and for whom further information was available) all were married. In almost all cases, they had been married a long time and had either two or three children. This finding may seem surprising if one thinks of very thick boundaries purely in terms of personal independence and distance from others; shouldn't the people with the thickest boundaries be living alone, away from others? It does make sense, however, in terms of a number of characteristics of thick-boundary people that I came to recognize in those I got to know well.

For one thing, people with thick boundaries tend to be very careful and well organized; thus they do not become involved in inappropriate relationships impulsively. The relationship is thought out, and entered into with care. When both partners act in this way, the results appear to be solid, or in any case lasting. Second, people with thick boundaries are very aware of the expectations of the group, class, and society. They tend to be on the conventional side, and to a greater-than-average degree their actions are guided by group pressures. Certainly the expectation, among much of our society, is that one will be married by a certain age and will have at least one child, preferably several children. Similarly there is pressure to stay married, if at all possible, although divorce is becoming common enough so that this expectation is far less strict than it was. My impression is that these people were, to an unusual degree, acting according to society's expectations (and often their family's expectations) in getting into and staying in long-term marriages. I do not mean to imply that the marriages were bad marriages; the ones I am thinking of seemed to function well, but there was a sense that the marriage relationship was simply accepted as part of the way the world was—part of the boundaries of one's world, perhaps—and the partners would usually remain with it whether or not they actively enjoyed the relationship or loved each other.

In some of these relationships, the thick-boundary people seemed not so much to have thinned their boundaries in joining another person but to have placed an additional thick boundary around the two of them, between them and the world. Usually a thick boundary continued to exist between the partners as well as around them: "My wife is my best friend, yet we are not particularly close."

Some of the people with thick boundaries had a remarkable capacity for getting along and living with others in peace. There was not much sense of closeness, but there was little conflict, or at least overtly expressed conflict. Sometimes, but not always, there seemed to be a defensive avoidance of conflict. Tom, the patient with the perfectly organized attaché case and one of the men who scored the thickest, lived with his parents until he was married at the age of twenty-nine. He was not especially passive or dependent, nor was he shy about meeting new people or unable to support himself financially. In fact, he had an excellent job and contributed to the family's finances. He did not feel particularly close to his parents; living at home was simply convenient: "I really liked my mother's cooking. It was convenient. We were all used to my living there; there didn't seem any reason to move out." I asked whether there were ever fights or disagreements. Tom said no, never. They got along fine; he lived his own life and didn't really see that much of his parents. They had dinner together, but they didn't talk much; eating was serious business in the family, and they all liked to eat. He knew that he and his father disagreed about a lot of things—politics, for example—but the disagreements never came up. "Why rock the boat?"

Another man with very thick boundaries was married to a woman who also appeared to have thick boundaries. They were intelligent, well-educated people who led an active social life, and they had four children whom they loved dearly. This couple could not be described as emotionally close—in fact, they tended to lead busy parallel lives—but they did enjoy a tranquility that most would envy. There were no major fights or disputes. The most significant disagreement between them during the years I was acquainted with them involved swimming. Both were avid athletes who occasionally swam in local competitions. At one point the husband hired a swimming coach, and his wife decided she could use some coaching too and planned to hire her own coach. The husband objected that this was a waste of money; why couldn't she share his coach? Some words, not excessively harsh, were exchanged, and that was it. The course of true love does seem to be running smooth here, though some might object that the somewhat distant love of the thick-boundary types is not the true love the poet had in mind.

People with very thin boundaries tend to become involved in relationships quickly, without the care, planning, and concern for the approval of others that so characterize the thick people just mentioned. They feel immediately attracted to someone: "She just felt right to me" or "The moment I saw him I had this powerful feeling that he was the man for me, and I always trust my feelings." They are the ultimate champions (and sometimes victims) of love at first sight. In friendships or other nonsexual relationships too, they are guided by an immediate feeling of closeness or trust. Lavinia, the woman mentioned in chapter 1 who could trust me because she saw a beautiful purple aura around me, went on to explain that she didn't especially like doctors or scientists, and she was prepared simply to walk out of the interview if I didn't feel right to her or had the wrong sort of aura.

Followed over time, the people with thin boundaries appeared to have intense but often short-lived relationships. They might fall madly in love, live only for that person and the relationship and be willing to follow the beloved to the ends of the earth, but then go through a traumatic breakup, with pain that long outlasted the relationship. Suicidal thoughts during these painful separations were not uncommon.

The thin-boundary people follow their feelings and impulses both in entering and in leaving relationships. They are much less influenced by social pressure or expectation—they do not remain married or in a relationship because others expect it—and their unhappiness can become so intense that when the relationship begins to feel wrong, they run. This tendency accounts for the finding that the people with very thin boundaries in our sample did not fall predominantly into any one marital status: they might be single, married, separated, or divorced, and they shifted rapidly from one category to another.

When two people with thin boundaries are married to each other or in a long-term relationship, the course of true love does not run smooth. They may feel intensely close and involved, but at times one or both will feel intensely hurt and rejected. One partner may try to pull away but find it difficult; they keep being drawn back together. The young artists in the opera *La Boheme* come to mind.

Of course I am again using the extreme thick and thin positions for emphasis; most people fall somewhere in between. Moreover, people can change, as we have seen. For example, people with very thin boundaries can sometimes learn to form firmer boundaries—to delay, to consider, to pay attention to factors besides their immediate feelings in this all-important interpersonal sphere.

It might be that a person with very thin boundaries would do better married to someone with very thick ones. This sort of relationship certainly happens; an artistic, somewhat flighty woman may marry a strong, solid man who will take care of her, or a male poet or painter may attach himself to a firm, motherly woman. But these relationships with well-defined but totally different, complementary roles seem somehow old-fashioned. They may have occurred more often when marriages were arranged or at least helped along, when some older relative could assess the situation and decide, "What he needs is someone like Jane." These days, such pairings seem rare. I can think of few definite instances among the many patients and research subjects I have seen, or among my friends. The very thin are not often attracted to the very thick: "He's solid, yes, but so dull, so rigid." And the thick, though sometimes attracted at first, are frightened by the emotionality and changeability of the thin: "too flaky."

As I look over these characteristics of relationships in the extreme boundary groups, I am increasingly convinced that at least with respect to interpersonal relationships, the most fortunate are those who have a mixture of boundaries, some thick and some thin. Perhaps the ideal is an ability to shift from one sort to another. Like most people, I am often attracted to extremes, yet in this area it seems appropriate to appreciate or even idealize the middle ground.

With regard to sex, my impression is that people with thin boundaries enjoy sexual activity more than those with thick boundaries. Some of those who scored very thin spoke as if they actually had more sensory receptors and had a more intense, more whole-body sexual experiences than most. Just possibly, there might be some truth to this; they are sensitive in so many ways that sexual arousal might be another aspect of their sensitivity. But certainly they are especially able to throw themselves into an experience, to experience it completely. This ability may be related to their tendency to enter into a story or fantasy or daydream so completely that they find it hard to come back to reality.

Thick-boundary people can certainly enjoy sex, too, but they are more likely to be bounded by the surrounding realities: how much time do we have? will the children hear us? or, in other situations, is it safe? what will this lead to? what will people think? They may as a result be less completely involved in the sexual activity itself.

BOUNDARIES AND GROUPS

One aspect of boundaries is the way one sees oneself in terms of larger entities—families, tribes, ethnic groups, nations. A person with very thick group boundaries identifies very solidly with a certain group: "I am an Irish Catholic," "I am an American." This identification strongly influences how the person thinks—not as an individual alone but to a great extent as part of a group. When faced with something new, this person will not only think, "How does this feel to me? How shall I react?" but may be even more aware of the ways in which the group is involved: "How am I expected (by the group) to act? How will this make us (the group) look?"

Someone with thick boundaries in this sense will also tend to see the rest of the world in terms of solid groups. A politician, for instance—and in my experience politicians often have fairly thick boundaries—will see the world in terms of the urban vote, the Black vote, the Ward 6 vote. Marketing executives likewise make use of groupings imposed on the world: affluent retirees, teenagers, traditional blue-collar workers, and so on.

In my experience, the person with really thick boundaries not only thinks of groups, classes, and other such divisions as important, but often doesn't even think about it at all, simply acting as if it were entirely obvious. "That's the way things are." Similarly, people with thick group boundaries are more likely to assume that another person's beliefs, thoughts, and feelings are related to that person's membership in a certain group. When someone at a party says to me, "You're a doctor, so of course you will say that . . ." or, "You scientists, of course, believe that . . ." this person almost invariably turns out to be someone with thick boundaries.

To people who have thin boundaries, although they may belong to a variety of groups, group membership is more incidental, not as important to their identity. Such people think and react more as individuals and pay less attention to how it looks to the group. They tend to avoid a solid group identification, preferring either no group at all or something large and amorphous: "I'm a citizen of the world." Nor do they find it congenial to divide the world into "voting blocks" or "markets." They will avoid situations and occupations that seem to require such thinking.

From the group's point of view, the person with thick group boundaries is often a more desirable recruit or group member. Such a person can be counted on to become a solid, reliable part of the group and adopt the group's standards. The person with thin boundaries will often be seen as a bit unreliable—a critic, a rebel, "not a team player."

I have oversimplified the situation by speaking of thick group boundaries as part of a total picture of thick boundaries in many or all senses. In some people this is definitely the case. It can also happen, however, that a person with extremely thick interpersonal boundaries may want to keep a certain distance from others and hardly become a group member at all. Conversely, I have seen people with very thin interpersonal boundaries who have a great tendency or need to become attached to others and join groups very freely. They may become active and involved group members, and they may develop close relationships with other group members, but in my experience they still do not develop the sense of a strong group boundary; they do not think in terms of "us versus them."

The dedicated followers of a cult may be an extreme

example of this phenomenon. Such people frequently have painfully thin boundaries in some senses—the boundaries related to identity, for instance—and seem to adopt a superthick group boundary as a shield or as a replacement for something they are missing. They can be considered "thins" who have temporarily become very "thick."

Obviously, many factors influence one's group membership and identification with the group. Frequently there is little choice. One may be born a Hindu untouchable in India or a poor peasant in Latin America. Accidents of birth and socioeconomic forces combine to make one a member of a certain group or class, regardless of one's individual personality. Members of an oppressed class or minority are especially likely to identify strongly with that group. In this situation, outside forces are so powerful that the individual's boundary structure hardly makes a difference in group identification. Whether they have thin boundaries, thick boundaries, or a mixture of thick and thin, they see the need to stand together as a group in order to obtain their rights.

In many situations, however, I believe that personality structure—specifically the structure of one's boundaries—is a significant determinant of group membership and of a sense of belonging to a group. These factors also influence the functioning of the group. Thus, the person with thin boundaries is more likely to feel uncomfortable in a group but can also be useful to a group in pointing out difficulties or inconsistencies, in making clear that not all members of the group are alike and that different viewpoints need to be considered even within the group.

People with thin boundaries can be seen as critics of the group as well as self-critics, and thorns in the side of the more committed group members. But a well-functioning and self-correcting group can certainly benefit from a mixture of people with thin and thick boundaries. Having only thick-boundary members may tend to make a group too self-satisfied or self-righteous, and perhaps dangerous in this way. A group with too many thin-boundary members, on the other hand, will tend to be acrimonious and may fall apart.

In this chapter I have highlighted some of the ways our boundary structures affect and connect us in our relationships with others and as members of groups. We have briefly examined gender differences and choice of career (to be discussed further in chapter 11). These topics are all related strands, interwoven in many intricate patterns to produce the tapestry of one person's relationship with others. I have discussed here only the principal findings and impressions derived from my interviews and research data.

CHAPTER 8

Boundaries, Sleep, and Dreaming

WE STARTED, a number of chapters ago, with a discussion of nightmares, because it was a study of nightmare sufferers that originally led to our work on boundaries. Now that we have looked at the Boundary Questionnaire and some of the data the questionnaire has produced, it may be worthwhile to return to our starting point and examine the relationship of boundaries not only to nightmares but to dreams in general and to other aspects of the basic biological states of sleep and waking in which we spend our lives.

Sleep and waking are of course two basic well-recognized states. In recent years, however, research has identified two very different states within sleep: REM sleep, also known as D (desynchronized or dreaming) sleep, turns out to be physiologically quite distinct from the remainder of sleep, called NonREM or S (synchronized) sleep. In fact, REM sleep in many ways resembles waking more than it resembles NonREM sleep (Dement 1958; Jouvet 1962). Therefore we can now think of our bodies and minds as spending time in three basic states—waking, NonREM sleep, and REM sleep, when most dreaming occurs—and can try to relate boundary characteristics to these three states and the transitions between them.

BOUNDARIES AND DREAMING

Out of the first 1,100 persons who took the Boundary Questionnaire, 759 also filled out a one-page data sheet containing a few questions about occupation, age, marital status, and the like. It also asked several questions about sleep, including these:

> Hours of sleep on an average night ___________
>
> Frequency of remembered dreaming (per week) ___________
>
> How often do you experience a nightmare (long frightening dream that wakes you up)? ___________

When the answers to these three questions were correlated with SumBound, the overall thinness score, an important relationship between boundary structure and dreaming became clear. Although there was little overall correlation between thinness of boundaries and number of nightmares, a strong positive correlation was found between thinness and the frequency of remembered dreaming (table 4).

These findings are intriguing in several ways. First, the lack of a strong correlation between SumBound and number of nightmares is surprising, especially in view of the fact the large total sample included two small groups of subjects (containing a total of thirty-two subjects) who were chosen because they had frequent nightmares and who scored very thin (high SumBound). The overall lack of correlation suggests that these nightmare sufferers must have been outweighed or balanced by groups who had few or no nightmares and thin boundaries, groups who had nightmares but thick boundaries, or both. Examination of the data revealed that there were indeed a great many subjects who had thin boundaries but few or no nightmares. In fact, as other studies (for example, Hartmann 1984) have found, most adults reported no nightmares or only a few per year. From these data we can conclude that if one has a lot of nightmares one is

Table 4 Correlations of SumBound with Sleep and Dreaming ($N = 759$)

	Sleep Time (Hours per night)	*Dream Frequency (Dreams per week)*	*Nightmare Frequency (Nightmares per year)*
SumBound	$r = .17$*	$r = .40^{\dagger}$	$r = .06$
SumBound with all sleep/dream/wake questions removed	$r = .16$*	$r = .37^{\dagger}$	$r = .04$

*p < .01
†p < .0001

likely to have thin boundaries but that the converse is not true. One can have thin boundaries without having nightmares, and that combination is fairly common.

There were also a few people who reported frequent nightmares yet scored thick on the Boundary Questionnaire. In those cases where records were available, however, the circumstances turned out to be unusual: two of these subjects had narcolepsy, a medical sleep disorder involving sleep attacks in the daytime and often characterized by frequent dreams and nightmares; two had other unusual medical disorders; one was actually describing night terrors, not nightmares—a distinction that will be discussed later in this chapter—and one had experienced frequent nightmares only recently while taking a number of medications.

In contrast with the lack of overall correlation with nightmares, there was a highly significant ($r = .40$; $p < .0001$) correlation between thinness of boundaries and number of dreams recalled. I found this definite positive correlation surprising, because the dream recall information is poor, or "noisy," data, consisting of a quick answer to a single question that is not very carefully worded. One problem with the wording is that "frequency of remembered dreaming" does not specify whether we mean during the subject's whole lifetime, or this year, or perhaps just this week; because we are considering thick or thin boundaries as a long-term or lifelong feature of personality, we would like to relate them to long-term or lifelong patterns of dream recall, but the one-page data sheet did not make that clear, and some subjects may well have answered on the basis of their dream recall during the past few weeks. This problem and other "noise" or random variation in the data would make it harder to find a highly significant correlation such as we actually found between SumBound and dreaming.

The correlation between thinness and dream recall was even higher ($r = .56$) in one subgroup—forty-two members of the Association for the Study of Dreams—consisting of people especially interested in their dreams. These people would be likely to answer the question "frequency of remembered dreaming (per week)" most carefully and would be likely to realize it referred to long-term patterns of recall.

One concern was that this interesting relationship might be tautological: the Boundary Questionnaire or parts of it, might be worded in such a way that someone with considerable dream recall would be likely to score thin. Indeed the Boundary Questionnaire does contain several questions related to dreaming, such as "In my dreams people sometimes merge into each other or become other people." Someone who remembers a great many dreams is more likely to have had this experience than someone who seldom remembers dreaming. To eliminate this problem, we ran the correlation again eliminating these questions; in fact, we eliminated not only questions about dreams but the entire category of questions dealing with sleep, waking, dreams, nightmares, daydreams, and reverie (fourteen questions). The correlation with SumBound was still highly significant ($r = .37$; $p < .0001$) and almost as high as before. It therefore appears likely that the relationship is a meaningful one.

We examined this relationship in a different way by

comparing frequent dreamers (seven or more dreams recalled per week) in our total sample with nondreamers (those who reported dreaming either "never" or "almost never"). The sixty-four frequent dreamers scored significantly higher than the sixty-nine nondreamers on SumBound: 314 +/− 60 for the dreamers versus 232 +/− 40 for the nondreamers. The dreamers also scored significantly higher on each of the twelve content categories of the Boundary Questionnaire (see Appendix, table A-4). One might have expected a difference on the sleep/dream/wake category and possibly on unusual experiences, but the frequent dreamers scored significantly thinner on such categories as neatness and precision, opinions about organizations, and opinions about truth and beauty. These relationships were not expected, but they confirmed the finding of a connection between frequent dream recall and thinness in general. In addition they provide further support for our thinking of thin and thick boundaries as one broad dimension, rather than unrelated pieces.

As I think about it in retrospect, the relationship between dream recall and thin boundaries makes a great deal of sense. After all, dream recall implies crossing a boundary. To recall a dream one must take an experience that occurred in one state (usually REM sleep) and transport it to a different state, waking; in other words, one must cross a kind of boundary. If boundary thickness is a meaningful measure in terms of so many boundaries in the mind, we should not be surprised to find that it is also related to boundaries between these basic states. Perhaps there are biological characteristics of REM sleep, NonREM sleep, and waking and of the transitions between them that differ in people with thick boundaries and people with thin boundaries. Some evidence for this idea will be discussed in chapter 12.

Dream recall is a complex phenomenon, and it is influenced not only by personality but by a number of physiological factors, by motivation, and by other factors (for reviews see Cohen 1974; Goodenough 1974; Belicki 1987). Relationships between dream recall and personality variables found in past studies have not always been replicated, so we will have to wait to see to what extent the relationship to boundaries holds up. On the basis of our large sample, however, it seems safe to say that boundary structure appears to bear some relationship to dream recall.

When dreams *are* recalled, is the content different in people with thick boundaries and people with thin ones? Do boundaries make a difference in how we dream and what we dream about? To answer these questions, we have collected and examined dreams from twenty subjects who scored either very thick or very thin on the Boundary Questionnaire and who were willing to come in for studies that included a detailed report of a recent dream. (We had planned to obtain information from five men and five women at each end of the continuum, but we ended up with eleven thin scorers—seven women and four men—and nine thick scorers—four women and five men.)

As would be expected, we found that it was harder to obtain dreams from the thick subjects; they were more likely to say that they had not had a dream in the past month. One dream was eventually obtained from each subject, and all dreams were rated on a blind basis by two independent judges on a number of rating scales that have been applied to dreams (Winget and Kramer 1979; Foulkes 1966). The judges agreed well, and overall the dreams of the thin group were rated as significantly more vivid, detailed, emotional, "dream-like," and bizarre, and with more interaction between characters.

In addition, the four groups of dreams (from thin men, thin women, thick men, and thick women) were given to four different judges who knew nothing about the groups. The judges were simply asked to say something about a group of dreams and what distinguished it from the other groups. The characterizations of the dreams of the two thin groups included such phrases as "a lot of emotional involvement," "intensity," "concern with interpersonal problems," "the dreamer is a victim." The thick dreams were characterized by phrases such as "little emotion," "lonely or barren scenes," "the dreamer is distant, not involved in the dream" (Hartmann, Elkin, and Garg, in press). These characterizations are interesting in that they are very consistent with how I might describe the waking mental content of the thin and thick patients I have seen in therapy. Clearly the very thick people, who find it hard to free-associate and talk about emotional problems, report dreams in the same way. As always in dream research, we cannot be certain whether their dream experiences are actually different from those of the thin subjects or whether the differences are mainly in their style of reporting the experience.

Following are two typical dreams, exactly as they were written by the dreamers. The first is from a woman who scores very thin:

> I was making a trip with my son. Our belongings were stacked high on a pickup truck type of vehicle. Our destination was blocked by a line of traffic which was bumper to bumper—lining both sides of a highway, both to and from our destination. The truck stalled in a railroad crossing, and my son and I pushed the vehicle over the crossing. The scene melted and transformed to a scene at the end of my destination where the president and his wife were seated at a set of tables, stacked haphazardly and covered with dust. I offered them coffee, and again the scene dissolved into the next room where my mother was emotionally tugging on me to meet her needs. I looked in the mirror which was misted and observed with horror that my eyes were injured with two fleshy pendants hanging from my irises. As I watched, the fleshy hangings increased in size and I awoke with my heart pounding with anxiety.

This dream was reported by Charles (chapter 5), a man who scored very thick:

> I was in a room, squarish in shape, with concrete walls on three sides. The fourth side was all glass or unglazed and open. The view seemed to be from inside the bottom of a large concrete dam looking out at the spillway some (undetermined) feet below. There were three of us in the room; two were college friends. We were joined by a fourth person, whose name I don't now recall, who came toward us from what seemed like a long, small, square concrete tunnel.

I cannot discuss these dreams and their meanings for the dreamers in detail here, but one could certainly say that simply in their manifest content the two dreams differ along the dimensions I have discussed. In addition there is a hint that in these two dreams the images actually depict the dreamer's type of boundaries. The man's dream is full of solid structures, walls, concrete. I have had two patients in therapy who themselves noted how often their dreams involved walls, fences, or thick rectangular structures. In the woman's dream, the dream scenes dissolve and change, and in the last scene her own face is changing shape in a frightening manner.

Here is an even more dramatic example from a woman who scored very thin:

> My father skinned me with a knife just the way one skins a rabbit. He skinned me and my sisters, and threw us in a heap. I was lying there with no skin, quivering, bloody; it was horribly painful, I could feel everything.

Boundaries thus appear to be related to dreams in several important ways. Having thick or thin boundaries correlates with the amount of dream recall and also with the qualities of the remembered dreams, the degree to which they are "dream-like, vivid, emotional, or bizarre." And it is possible that boundaries enter into dream content, so that one sometimes dreams about the state of one's boundaries.

Finally, thinking about dreaming more theoretically, one could describe dreaming as an extremely thin-boundary state of mind. Dreaming contains vivid imagery not distinguished from reality; one image merges into another; past and present merge; images, thoughts, and feelings from different times in one's life all come together. *Condensation* (Freud's term), or bringing things together, is a hallmark of dreaming; there are few separations or boundaries. In other words, we all have thin boundaries when we are dreaming. One could say there is more difference between the waking and dreaming states in those who have thick boundaries and less difference in those with thin boundaries.

BOUNDARIES AND SLEEP

In the theoretical discussion of types of boundaries in chapter 2, I mentioned one sort of relationship between boundaries and sleep, the sharpness of the experienced dividing line. People who have thick boundaries in many senses tend to make a clean division: they are asleep or they're awake, period. They tend to wake up quickly in the morning and be wide awake at once; they do not ooze gradually from one state into another or spend time in in-between states. Very thin people do make slow transitions, and they spend considerable time in states that they may call dozing or reverie or daydreaming or simply lying there half asleep. This characteristic was so clear in our original groups of nightmare sufferers that it was incorporated as one question in the Boundary Questionnaire. And indeed this question—"When I awake in the morning, I am not sure whether I am really awake for a few minutes"—correlated well with SumBound ($r = .29$, $p < .001$), placing it in the highest 25 percent of item-total correlations.

An additional, very different sort of relationship is suggested by the correlations between SumBound and sleep time (table 4). There was a significant positive correlation between SumBound and length of sleep, although the relationship was not as strong as with dream recall.*

Although the relationship is not a powerful one, let us consider it seriously for a moment. Would it make any sense that people with thick boundaries might have a tendency to sleep less than the average, and people with thin boundaries to sleep more? If so, what could such a relationship mean? The correlation appears clearly in our nonpatient groups, so it is unlikely to be related to insomnia. Insomniacs are people who not only report short sleep hours but consider their sleep insufficient. But there is another sort of person who reports short sleep: the "short sleeper," who sleeps less than six hours per night but is perfectly content with this amount of sleep. Such people consider that they are getting all the sleep they need; they have no complaints and do not qualify as insomniacs. Our boundary-sleep correlation probably involves people with varying sleep needs, but who are relatively satisfied with their sleep.

The idea that people with thick boundaries might need or habitually obtain less sleep than most, or that having thin boundaries somehow increases the need for sleep, may not be entirely implausible. In fact, it may be consistent with some data on personality characteristics of long and short sleepers. Only a few such studies exist.

*Statisticians will be quick to point out that a correlation of .17, although highly significant in this group of seven hundred—unlikely to be a chance occurrence—is nonetheless not a close relationship; it accounts for only a very small fraction (.029) of the total variance. What this means in practical terms is the fairly obvious fact that many other variables besides boundary score determine a person's sleep time; one cannot make much of a guess at someone's sleep time if one knows nothing but his or her boundary score, and vice versa.

Studies examining groups of long and short sleepers among college students found no clear differences (Webb and Agnew 1970), but the students' sleeping habits were not truly habitual; those who had reported sleeping six hours a night or nine hours a night reported very different lengths of sleep a year later (Webb 1979). Studies in my laboratory, however, involved people with more regular longstanding patterns of long or short sleep and demonstrated a number of personality differences.

These studies were part of a series of investigations of the functions of sleep (Hartmann 1973; Hartmann et al. 1971). The idea was that if there were people who did not need any sleep, one could learn about what sleep does for us by looking at differences between those people and others who do need to sleep. There appears to be no one who does not need any sleep, however, so the best we could do was to study people who need much less sleep than most—we did find a large number of peope who never needed more than six hours of sleep—and compare them with average sleepers and with people who seemed to need more sleep than most—more than nine hours per day. We accepted only those who stated that their pattern had lasted at least a year (usually it had lasted their entire adult lives) and who kept a sleep log showing that they stuck to their reported pattern every day for two weeks. Our studies involved sleep laboratory recordings as well as interviews and psychological tests, including the MMPI. Information was obtained on a total of 227 long and short sleepers, of whom 29 went through a complete series of eight nights in the sleep laboratory.

The laboratory studies need not concern us here, but the findings from the interviews, questionnaires, and psychological tests are of interest. Several statistically significant differences were found between the long- and short-sleeper groups: the short sleepers became alert more quickly in the morning, reported dreaming less at home (1.7 dreams per week versus 3.1 dreams per week for the long sleepers), and scored significantly higher on the L scale of the MMPI, compared with the long sleepers. In a summary of the interviews, the short sleepers were described as

> efficient, energetic, ambitious persons who tended to work hard and to keep busy. They were relatively sure of themselves, socially adept, decisive, and were satisfied with themselves and their lives. They had few complaints either about the study, about their life situations, or about politics and the state of the world. They were somewhat conformist in their social and political views, and they wished to appear very normal and "All-American." They were extroverted and definitely were not "worriers"; they seldom left themselves time to sit down and think about problems; in fact several of them, on being asked what they did in times of stress and worry, made statements such as "I never let my worries go to my head." (Hartmann et al. 1972, p. 467)

These short sleepers obviously have a great many similarities with our very-thick-boundary subjects. The Boundary Questionnaire was not available at the time of the long- and short-sleeper study, but looking back at my notes on individuals in that study, I have little question that the short sleepers would have scored relatively thick.

The long sleepers from that study were noted to be

"less easily definable"; they were described as "worriers," and a few of them were creative or artistic. As I look over the published reports as well as my interview notes, however, I do not see a very obvious correspondence between the long sleepers and our present subjects who scored very thin on the Boundary Questionnaire. Some of the long sleepers definitely appear to me to have thin boundaries; some of them might score around the midrange; in some I cannot even hazard a guess. In any case there does appear to be some possible relationship between boundaries and habitual sleep or sleep requirement, at least a relationship between having a low sleep requirement and having thick boundaries.

Our studies also related to possible functions of sleep. In view of the fact that people who are "efficient, decisive, satisfied, nonworriers," whom we also described as "preprogrammed,"* appear to need much less sleep than the "worriers" and "reprogrammers," we suggested that sleep may have a role in some kind of restoration after worry or reprogramming. Consistent with this conclusion were the results of our studies of "variable sleepers," people who reported having changed their sleep needs or having variable sleep needs, requiring much more sleep at certain times of their lives than at others. We found that these subjects, during their periods (months or years) of low sleep need, somewhat resembled the habitual short sleepers—they were efficient,

*Using a computer analogy, we also described the short sleepers as "preprogrammed." They seemed to have basic ways of doing things ("programs") for their lives, which were working well and were seldom changed. Their lives were going in a straight line. The long sleepers were not as satisfied and kept changing their plans and approaches to life. They were called "reprogrammers," and their lives involved a lot of zigzags.

energetic nonworriers—and during periods of high sleep need resembled the habitual long sleepers (Hartmann 1973; Hartmann and Brewer 1976).

This discussion has taken us some distance from boundaries. It may be important, however, that people with thick boundaries may tend to need less sleep than most and in some ways resemble the "non-worrier, preprogrammed" short sleepers. We will return to this in the last chapter.

SLEEP DISORDERS

About three hundred patients seen at our sleep disorders center have taken the Boundary Questionnaire, providing us with some insights into the boundary characteristics of people with a variety of sleep disorders. Sleep disorders, especially the several forms of insomnia, are common conditions, affecting almost one-third of the adult population every year. Among those who took the questionnaire, we have large enough groups for discussion in several diagnostic categories: sleep apnea, nocturnal myoclonus (muscle jerks), bruxism (nocturnal tooth-grinding), nightmares, night terrors/sleepwalking, and several kinds of insomnia. (For a review of these and other sleep disorders, see Kryger, Roth, and Dement 1989.) Some of the sleep disorders, such as obstructive sleep apnea, are clear-cut physical illnesses, and we would not expect any particular relationship to a personality dimension such as thick and thin boundaries. Others, such as the insomnias, have psychological as well as physical aspects and could show some relationships to boundaries that might help us in classifying and understanding the disorders.

Obstructive sleep apnea, a repeated cessation of breathing during sleep, has been described and studied only in the past twenty years, yet it turns out to be a fairly common as well as very serious sleep disorder. The problem involves repeated closure of the airway during sleep, at the pharyngeal level. The most common symptoms and signs of apnea are loud snoring at night and daytime sleepiness. Patients characteristically have thick necks and may be overweight. Among the sleep-disorder patients who took the Boundary Questionnaire were forty-four patients with obstructive sleep apnea. In most cases there was no associated psychiatric diagnosis. SumBound for these patients averaged 223 +/− 30. This score is on the thick side, but the group was older than our average and included more males than females; applying corrections for age and sex, the total boundary score was 241 +/− 30, still significantly thicker than the overall average of 273 +/− 52.

The same is true of nocturnal myoclonus, now often called periodic limb movements of sleep (PLS), a condition characterized by repetitive muscle jerks, sometimes several hundred times per night and sometimes producing severe sleep disturbance. A total of twenty-eight patients with a diagnosis of nocturnal myoclonus took the Boundary Questionnaire, and again the boundary scores were somewhat thicker than average (258 +/− 41, corrected for sex and age).

I have no certain explanation for the somewhat thick boundary scores found in patients with apnea and myoclonus; there is no reason to think that someone with thick boundaries would be predisposed to develop these particular medical conditions. There might possibly be an effect in the opposite direction, however: apnea and myoclonus can be, and were in these patients, serious long-term conditions that not only disrupt sleep but interfere with waking activity by producing profound daytime sleepiness, lethargy, and feelings of depression. Many patients feel they must fight against these feelings with all their strength in order to continue functioning. This sort of long-term stress may lead to a thickening of boundaries, as discussed in chapter 6.

Bruxism is usually less serious, but it is an interesting and quite common condition. It is characterized by powerful grinding of the teeth during sleep; the sound is sometimes loud enough to awaken a person in the next room, although the patient remains asleep. The grinding can severely damage the teeth, but it is a problem mainly seen by dentists; patients with bruxism seldom come to a sleep disorders center, and we did not see many there. We did, however, conduct an entire research project specifically devoted to bruxism, in which twenty-two subjects took part. Sixteen of the subjects were studied for four nights each in the sleep laboratory, where we investigated details of the bruxism and demonstrated that in some people it was aggravated by alcohol use (Hartmann et al. 1987a). All the subjects filled out the Boundary Questionnaire; the average SumBound score, corrected for age and sex, was 237 +/− 39, again considerably thicker than average.

Is there any reason why thick boundaries might be related to this dental disorder? Bruxism, unlike apnea and myoclonus, does not usually disrupt sleep greatly and has little effect on waking functioning; thus I would not consider it a source of long-term stress. There may, however, be a different sort of connection. Muscular tension is one of the factors that may contribute to bruxism, and muscular tension in turn may be related to personality; psychological factors, especially repressed anger or hostility, have also sometimes been thought to contribute to bruxism (Molin and Levi 1966). In our study a few of the patients with bruxism could be given the psychiatric diagnosis of obsessive-compulsive personality disorder, and a number of others had some features of it; we concluded that the group could be characterized as "somewhat obsessional, perfectionistic, and tightly controlled, with some difficulty in handling emotions, especially anger, at times of stress" (Hartmann et al. 1987b, p. 350). Thus it is at least possible that people with thick boundaries, who as we have seen often have some obsessive-compulsive traits, who use powerful defenses such as repression and isolation, and who do not easily let emotional material into their associations (or even into their dreams), might on this basis have more of a tendency than others to develop bruxism.

Nightmares have already been discussed at length; we have seen that people with frequent nightmares turned out to have very thin boundaries. The people in the study were subjects volunteering for research projects, however, not patients in treatment at a sleep disorders center. People do not often come to a sleep disorders center with a chief complaint of nightmares, but we do now have seven such patients who came in specifically because they were having nightmares. This group scored 313 +/− 90 on the Boundary Questionnaire, much thinner than average and no different from the research subjects with nightmares. It appears that having frequent nightmares is associated with having thin boundaries, whether or not one sees the nightmares as a disorder requiring help.

Night terrors are frequently confused with nightmares, but they are a very different phenomenon. Night terrors are not frightening dreams but rather early-night, usually dreamless attacks in which the sleeper awakens in terror, sometimes with a scream, sometimes with a movement or an episode of sleepwalking. Physiologically, too, they are different: they arise not from long REM-periods but from partial awakenings out of deep early sleep and are associated with huge increases in pulse and respiratory rates.

Are night terrors also experienced by people with unusual boundary structures? It appears so. Among our sleep disorders patients, we had sixteen cases of night terrors or night terrors combined with sleep walking. Their average corrected SumBound scores were 238 +/− 44, much thicker than the scores of the nightmare sufferers and in fact significantly thicker than the overall average. And night terror sufferers have been found to differ from nightmare sufferers in many ways (Hartmann 1984).

Finally, we can consider insomnia, or rather the broad group of insomnias. Insomnia—difficulty in falling asleep or staying asleep—is the most common symptom related to sleep, but one must keep in mind that it is a symptom, not an illness. Insomnia, like a stomach ache, can have many underlying causes. This fact is important in terms of treatment; one should not simply treat a symptom ("You can't sleep? Take a sleeping pill.") but rather try to determine and treat the cause. Among the many causes of insomnia are purely physical causes such as sleep apnea and nocturnal myoclonus; substances such as medications or alcohol; psychiatric causes such as depression and anxiety; and environmental causes such as jet lag (Hartmann 1978; Karacan et al. 1988; Kryger, Roth, and Dement 1989).

Thus insomnia is such a broad term that we could hardly expect all insomniacs to have one sort of boundary structure. And in fact, SumBound in our group of over one hundred insomniacs (267 +/− 49) was very close to the overall average. In my clinical work with insomniacs, however, I have been struck by the fact that some of them appeared to have very thick and others quite thin boundaries. Could there be an underlying pattern?

To answer this question, I examined the data in our samples in two different ways. First I read through the clinical charts of the twenty subjects at each end of the overall boundary distribution, for whom information was available, to get an idea of whether insomnia occurred, and what kind, in very thick or very thin subjects. In the very thick group, there were eight patients who complained of insomnia. In five of these, the probable diagnosis (cause of the insomnia) was nocturnal myoclonus. Two of the five were also noted to be tense or obsessive-compulsive, and one was depressed; these might have been contributory causes of the insomnia. The other three had no medical cause for the insomnia; in all three the diagnosis was psychophysiological insomnia, to be described in more detail below, and all had some features of obsessive-compulsive personality disorder.

Insomnia was also common in the very thin group; thirteen of the twenty complained of insomnia as at least one of their presenting symptoms. In this group, however, the diagnoses, or underlying causes, were very different. None of these patients had nocturnal myoclonus, sleep apnea, or other clear medical cause for insomnia, and none had a diagnosis of psychophysiological insomnia or obsessive-compulsive personality disorder. The most common diagnosis was insomnia secondary to a psychiatric condition, with varying underlying conditions: borderline personality disorder, schizotypal personality disorder, generalized anxiety disorder, dysthymic disorder (chronic depression), and mixed personality disorder. A number of patients were noted to be "unusually sensitive" or "fragile" without a definite diagnosis.

It is noteworthy that both extreme boundary groups contained a number of insomniacs but that the causes for the insomnia appeared to be very different. In the thick group the cause was most often a medical condition (nocturnal myoclonus), psychophysiological insomnia, or obsessive-compulsive personality disorder. In the thin group the cause was not thought to be a purely medical condition in any of the thirteen cases; the insomnia appeared to be related to psychological factors, but with no single dominant diagnosis.

After examining these data on the very-thick-boundary and very-thin-boundary groups, I went back to the large group of insomniacs in our sleep disorders data file and obtained boundary scores on individuals with certain diagnoses that appeared to be of interest. A sizable group of patients had been given the diagnosis of psychophysiological insomnia. This fairly common but incompletely understood condition involves sleeplessness related not only to patterns of increased tension and arousal in the body but to conditioned factors: bed becomes a place associated with being restless, tense, or angry about not sleeping, rather than a place where one sleeps. Patients with this diagnosis usually have no clear psychiatric diagnosis, but they are often described as tense and sometimes as rigid or perfectionistic; thus they have some of the characteristics of obsessive-compulsive personality. The group with this diagnosis turned out to have a corrected SumBound score of 251 +/− 45 on the Boundary Questionnaire, considerably thicker than average.

There was only a small group—six insomniacs—who received the diagnosis of insomnia secondary to the specific psychiatric diagnosis of obsessive-compulsive personality disorder. These patients also scored relatively thick on the Boundary Questionnaire: SumBound was 258 +/− 53.

Thus two subgroups of insomniacs had definitely thick boundaries. Moreover, in these patients certain aspects of thick boundaries may actually have played a part in producing the insomnia. Many of them, according to our interview notes, were saying to themselves, in one way or another, "I've *got* to sleep; I'll just try harder and *make* myself sleep"; that, of course, is not an effective way to get to sleep. Others felt, "I've got to do everything perfectly, and that includes getting to sleep." These attitudes, which are characteristic of active waking and involve maintaining control and perfectionism, often produced sleeplessness rather than sleep.

I also examined the data to determine whether we had groups in which the diagnosis was insomnia secondary to schizotypal personality disorder, borderline personality disorder, or other disorders—patients in whom we might expect to find thin boundaries. I found only very small groups, containing three or four patients each, for these specific diagnoses, so it did not make sense to analyze these separately. We were, however, able to form one large mixed group of patients diagnosed as having insomnia secondary to other psychiatric conditions (other, meaning all except obsessive-compulsive personality disorder). Adjusted for age and sex, this group scored 275 +/− 54, very close to the overall average but significantly thinner than the other insomniacs we have discussed. These patients did not have perfectionistic attitudes toward sleep. Their insomnia was often related to anxieties, worries, or concerns of various kinds; in some of them physical sensitivities to sound or light also played a part. And of course the small group with nightmares already mentioned sometimes complained of insomnia produced by their nightmares, and that group had the highest (thinnest) boundary scores.

Thus it appears that people with very different boundary structures become insomniac, although they may arrive there by different paths and develop different sorts of insomnia, which in turn require different treatments. It is possible that this situation—different paths related to boundary structure leading to similar symptoms—may be found in other medical and psychological conditions. This will be discussed further in the next chapter.

I have devoted an entire chapter to the relationships between boundaries and the spectrum of sleeping-dreaming-waking and sleep disorders not only because of my own interest in these topics but also because some of our most basic boundaries are involved. We spend our entire lives in the biological states of waking, NonREM sleep, and REM sleep, which roughly correspond to our sense of waking, dreamless sleep, and dreaming, and in the transitions between them. I believe that perhaps the most interesting findings, which need to be studied further, are those demonstrating greater dream recall in people with thin boundaries—perhaps as part of their general tendency to transfer easily between states, and to experience in-between states. This suggests, for instance, that one might explore the biology of boundaries (chapter 12) through the biology of dreaming and waking.

CHAPTER 9

Boundaries and Health

IN THIS CHAPTER we will explore the relationship of boundaries to health and illness. We will investigate whether people with different boundary structures differ in their vulnerability to illness and whether they develop different physical or mental illnesses, or different symptoms of the same illness. Finally, we will consider boundaries and the ways we deal with stress of many kinds.

PHYSICAL ILLNESS

If boundaries in a broad sense include protection against the world, might thick boundaries in some way serve as protection against illness? Might people with thick boundaries become ill less frequently than others, or be less vulnerable to certain kinds of physical illness? It seems farfetched but not impossible. One could postulate that the immune system, a barrier against many kinds of disease and closely related to the nervous system, might be more solid in some people than others, possibly related to the other boundaries we have been discussing, the boundaries in the mind. For example, could a certain kind of thick-boundary mindset—"I'm not vulnerable; I'm tough; I'm armor-plated; I'm a person who just doesn't get ill"—transmit itself to the body's immune systems or other defense systems and actually produce a reduction in illness? Or could it be that thick-boundary people and thin-boundary people actually have the same number of illnesses of the same severity but that those with thin boundaries experience their illness more intensely, feeling more pain and distress because they tend to be more sensitive?

One could also legitimately suggest the opposite conclusion: that those with thick boundaries might have more illness or more severe illness. One might, for example, assume that those with thin boundaries are accustomed to a variety of small pains and discomfort; they have adapted to their sensitive state and learned to live with these minor illnesses, accepting them as part of everyday life. On the other hand, those with thick boundaries may expect to be invulnerable and perfectly healthy, so that when some illness does strike them, they totally collapse, like the oak that refuses to bend in the wind.

The considerable literature on what has been called psychosomatic illness or psychophysiological aspects of illness (for a review, see, for example, Weiner 1977) suggests that psychological factors and personality factors can play a role in physical illness of many kinds, but the exact mechanisms are not known; these studies, of course, did not use measures of boundary structure.

As yet a study of boundaries and physical illness based on objective data from the Boundary Questionnaire is only in its early stages, but here again an examination of the subjects at the extreme ends of the thickness-thinness spectrum has proved fruitful. I examined in detail the patterns of illness and responses to an illness questionnaire, whenever it was available, in the individuals who scored thickest and thinnest on the Boundary Questionnaire. Here a pattern did emerge: The very thin group reported significantly more symptoms of illness, both in interviews and on a questionnaire called the Cornell Index (Weider et al. 1944), which consists of 101 questions about symptoms of various kinds—gastrointestinal, respiratory, and cardiovascular—including stress-related bodily symptoms. Many of the symptoms also relate to anxiety and depression, so that one cannot distinguish purely physical from more psychological problems (and in fact this is never easy to do.)

At the thick end of the entire population (approximately the 10 percent who scored thickest) there were twenty-two who had taken the Cornell Index: their average total score was 8.1 +/− 10.3. (The total score on the Cornell Index corresponds roughly to the total number of symptoms reported; the normal range is considered to be 0 to 8 or 0 to 10, in different situations.) Thus, a majority of these people scored in the normal range even though most of them had taken the Cornell Index because they had a problem, often a sleep disorder. At the thin end of the distribution, there were fourteen who had taken the Cornell Index: these subjects scored 28.4 +/− 18.0, far higher than average. The difference is highly significant and indicates that the thin subjects report more symptoms of illness than the thick subjects. Since many of the questions deal with severity of symptoms rather than only their presence, it appears that at least subjectively the people with thin boundaries have more severe complaints. There was no specific symptom or group of symptoms or type of illness that clearly differentiated the two groups. The differences were widespread: the thin-scoring subjects reported having a great variety of symptoms. It is noteworthy that there was not a single symptom reported more often by the group with thick boundaries. Overall it appears that people with very thin boundaries definitely report having symptoms of illness more than do those with thick boundaries. Whether they actually have more illness in an objective sense is not certain.

MENTAL ILLNESS

We have already discussed evidence for at least some relationship between boundaries and mental disorder. For example, two of the twenty thickest scorers on the Boundary Questionnaire could be given a diagnosis of obsessive-compulsive personality disorders. Among the thinnest scorers several could be diagnosed as borderline personality disorder or schizotypal personality disorder. It may now be useful to examine this possible relationship from the other direction—starting with patients who have a diagnosable mental disorder and examining their boundary scores and boundary characteristics.

Mental disorders in adults are currently classified by the official manual of the American Psychiatric Association, *Diagnostic and Statistical Manual of Mental Disorders* (DSM-IIIR) into two main groupings: Axis I, the clinical disorders, which can usually be thought of as mental illnesses, and Axis II, the personality disorders.

Personality Disorders

I shall first discuss the personality disorders, which might be expected to have a clearer relationship with a personality dimension or trait such as thick or thin boundaries. The definition of personality disorders is in fact based on the concept of personality trait. In effect, a personality disorder is an exaggerated, disturbing version of a personality trait. DSM-IIIR describes the difference:

> Personality traits are enduring patterns of perceiving, relating to, and thinking about the environment and oneself, and are exhibited in a wide range of important social and personal contexts. It is only when personality traits are inflexible and maladaptive and cause either significant functional impairment or subjective distress that they constitute "Personality Disorders." (p. 335)

The following are the currently recognized personality disorders:

Antisocial personality disorder
Avoidant personality disorder
Borderline personality disorder
Dependent personality disorder
Histrionic personality disorder
Narcissistic personality disorder
Obsessive-compulsive personality disorder
Paranoid personality disorder
Passive-aggressive personality disorder
Schizoid personality disorder
Schizotypal personality disorder

Because these are not well-defined illnesses but rather maladaptive ways of dealing with the world, there is always some difficulty in deciding just when the line into "inflexible and maladaptive" behavior has been crossed. There is also some overlap between the disorders: a person's "enduring patterns" may be maladaptive in several ways. Therefore psychiatrists and psychologists are never in perfect agreement regarding these diagnoses. The names give a rough indication of the content of each. I shall not discuss them all here but rather focus on those for which we have reason to suspect a relationship to boundaries.

There are two personality disorders whose definitions suggest some relationship to thin boundaries: borderline personality disorder and schizotypal personality disorder. Borderline personality disorder, according to DSM-IIIR, is

> a pervasive pattern of instability of self-image, interpersonal relationships, and mood, beginning by early adult-

> hood and present in a variety of contexts. A marked and persistent identity disturbance is almost invariably present. This is often pervasive, and manifested by uncertainty about several life issues, such a self-image, sexual orientation, long-term goals or career choice, type of friends or lovers to have, or which values to adopt. (p. 346)

Laura, whom we met in chapter 6, qualifies for this diagnosis.

Many of the characteristics listed sound familiar. Just reading this description would certainly lead one to predict that people with a diagnosis of borderline personality disorder would score thin on a measure of boundaries. And in fact Andrea Celenza (1986) did find thin scores on the Boundary Questionnaire in a group of eight patients with that diagnosis whom she studied intensively. This group had SumBound scores of 313 +/− 59, far above the overall mean of 273 and in the range of the art students and nightmare sufferers.

Among our large overall sample of patients who had taken the Boundary Questionnaire and for whom additional clinical files were available (mostly from the sleep disorders center), we found nine others in whom we had made the clinical diagnosis of borderline personality disorder. These patients scored 308 +/− 64 on the Boundary Questionnaire, again significantly thinner than our average. They scored especially thin on factor I (primary process thinking), factor IV (fragility), and factor VII (lack of organized planfulness) but thicker than average on factor IX (indicating a lack of flexibility). Thus there is little question that some relationship exists in the expected direction. This does not mean that people with thin boundaries suffer from borderline personality disorder. In fact, of the twenty extremely thin individuals profiled in chapter 5, only one could definitely be given this diagnosis, although others showed some features of it.

The description of schizotypal personality disorder again suggests a relationship with thin boundaries:

> a pervasive pattern of peculiarities of ideation, appearance and behavior and deficits in interpersonal relatedness, beginning by early adulthood and present in a variety of contexts, that are not severe enough to meet the criteria for schizophrenia. . . . The disturbance may include paranoid ideation, suspiciousness, . . . odd beliefs, magical thinking that is inconsistent with subcultural norms. . . . Examples include superstitiousness, beliefs in clairvoyance, telepathy. . . . Unusual perceptual experience may include illusions, sensing the presence of a force or person not actually present. . . . Concepts may be expressed unclearly or oddly, or words may be used in unusual ways. (DSM-IIIR, p. 340)

This definition is quite broad and could apply to many people who could best be described as eccentric, or a bit unusual. Lavinia, for example, who saw auras around people, met many of the criteria for schizotypal personality disorder. As with all the personality disorders, the diagnosis should be used only when the condition is "inflexible and maladaptive," causing "functional impairment or subjective distress" (DSM-IIIR, p. 335).

Among our large mixed sample of people who took the Boundary Questionnaire, there were seven who had been given a clinical diagnosis of schizotypal personality disorder. They scored 325 +/− 76 on the Boundary

Questionnaire, which is again in the very thin range, even thinner than those with borderline personality disorder. They scored especially thin on factor I (primary process), factor III (identification with children), and factor IV (fragility), but thick on factor II (preference for explicit boundaries) and factor VI (indicating a lack of trustful openness).

In another study, Ross Levin (1986) found a significant positive correlation between thin boundaries and high scores on two different scales designed to measure schizotypal personality. His findings are consistent with ours, but not precisely the same; his subjects were sixty college students, with and without nightmares, for whom no clinical psychiatric diagnoses had been made.

Here again the relationship between thin boundaries and schizotypal personality disorder does not imply that people with thin boundaries should generally be diagnosed as having schizotypal personality disorder. Of the twenty subjects who scored thinnest in our sample, four could be given this diagnosis.

The only personality disorder on the list that might appear to be related to thick boundaries is obsessive-compulsive personality disorder. In the official description

> the essential feature of this disorder is a pervasive pattern of perfectionism and inflexibility, beginning by early adulthood and present in a variety of contexts. . . . Work and productivity are prized to the exclusion of pleasure and interpersonal relationships. Often there is a preoccupation with logic and intellect and intolerance of affective behavior in others. . . . People with this disorder tend to be exces-

> sively conscientious, moralistic, scrupulous, and judgmental of self and others. (DSM-IIIR, pp. 354–355)

This definition, like the others, is quite broad, and it is sometimes hard to decide when a true disorder is present, rather than a personality trait. Many of the characteristics are suggestive of some of our findings in people with very thick boundaries. In fact, in our large sample, we had a total of thirty-three persons who could be diagnosed as obsessive-compulsive personality disorder, and they scored 243+/−46 on the Boundary Questionnaire—much lower (thicker) than average. They scored especially thick on factors I, indicating little primary process thinking, and factor IX, indicating lack of flexibility. Again this does not mean that anyone with thick boundaries can be given this diagnosis. Of our twenty extremely thick scorers, only two could be given a definite diagnosis of obsessive-compulsive personality disorder. Most of the people who scored very thick on the Boundary Questionnaire had solid family lives, held good jobs, and gave no evidence of obvious psychological illness or problems. In fact, their reliability, solidity, and good organizational skills (and perhaps just a touch of obsessiveness) often gave them an advantage in their careers. They did, however, have some complaints of a fairly consistent kind:

"I'm good at what I do, but I'm in a rut; I'd like to get out, but I'm not sure I'd be as good at anything else."
"I don't think I enjoy life as much as some people do."

"When I take a vacation, I seem to work at having a good time; it's just like being at work."
"I'd like to change my career, or change something in my life, but I can't see outside of it; there's a wall!"
"I'm like a billiard ball limited by the sides of the table!"

These exact quotes again demonstrate a relationship between thick boundaries and at least some aspects of obsessive-compulsive personality disorder. Some of these people are actually complaining of thick boundaries in the sense of walls around them!

None of the other personality disorders are defined in a way to suggest there would be a strong relationship to thick or thin boundaries, and the limited data in our samples do not suggest any relationship either.

Clinical Disorders

There is little reason to believe that most mental disorders and illnesses bear any definite relationship to thin and thick boundaries. We have seen repeatedly that having very thin or very thick boundaries does not mean that one is ill or crazy. Nonetheless a few conditions may be worth discussing in terms of possible tendencies or vulnerabilities.

For several reasons, I consider it possible that having thin boundaries may be related to a tendency to develop schizophrenia or a schizophreniform disorder. (The term *schizophreniform disorder* refers to an episode of the same sort of psychosis as schizophrenia—that is, it involves thought disorder as well as mood disorder—but one that lasts for less than six months; in other words, it is a brief schizophrenia-like episode.) First, a patient in the early phases of a schizophrenic or schizophreniform illness often describes some very thin-boundary experiences:

"There's too much coming in at me; I can't take it any more."

"It was beautiful at first. I could see so much at once, it seemed I could appreciate the world in a whole new way, but now it's scary, there's too much. I want to close my eyes and close my ears, but it doesn't stop."

"I don't know what's real anymore and what I'm just imagining."

Some detailed clinical descriptions of this situation can be found in Malcolm Bowers' *Retreat from Sanity* (1970).

Second, the small groups with a diagnosis of schizophrenia or schizophreniform disorder that we have studied so far did score relatively high (thin) on the Boundary Questionnaire. In our large sample, only six had a definite diagnosis of schizophrenia; these had a SumBound score of 305 +/− 41, definitely on the thin side. In addition, four of the patients with diagnoses of borderline or schizotypal personality disorder had experienced psychotic episodes and had been given the additional diagnosis of schizophreniform disorder; all four scored above 310 on the Boundary Questionnaire.

Furthermore, the diagnosis of *schizotypal personality dis-*

order was in fact derived from studies of relatives of schizophrenic patients (Kety et al. 1975). As we have seen, patients with this diagnosis too scored very thin on the Boundary Questionnaire.

My work on nightmare sufferers also suggests a relationship between thin boundaries and a tendency toward schizophrenia. As we have seen, these people had extremely thin boundaries. I found that a small number were themselves schizophrenic, and a larger number had a few of the symptoms of schizophrenia (Hartmann 1984; Hartmann et al. 1981). In a study of vulnerability to schizophrenia that involved people who had been followed for thirty years since their childhoods, we found that "permeable boundaries" in childhood was one of the indicators that predicted which children developed schizophrenia as adults (Hartmann et al. 1984). Permeable boundaries included such things as "excessive daydreaming" and "easily distracted." I would now call these aspects of thin boundaries.

Finally, among the MMPI scales that correlate well with thinness of boundaries are Pa (paranoia) and Sc (schizophrenia). These are exactly the scales elevated in most schizophrenic patients, although as we discussed they can be elevated in other conditions as well.

From all this one can conclude that there must be some relationship between thin boundaries and the schizophrenia-spectrum disorders. Patients with these disorders certainly tend to have thin boundaries, although as I have stressed, it is not the case that anyone with very thin boundaries is likely to be schizophrenic, or even vulnerable to schizophrenia.

Is there any mental illness that tends to be associated

with thick boundaries? One might expect the answer to be no; as we have seen, even people with very thick boundaries usually score normally on tests such as the MMPI, and they report few symptoms of any kind on questionnaires such as the Cornell Index. One might therefore expect people with thick boundaries to have less mental illness than others, and in fact, among the large sample I studied, the great majority of the people who scored very thick had no diagnosable mental illness of any kind. Even among the twenty thickest scorers there were only two with any diagnosable condition, and this was not a mental illness but obsessive-compulsive personality disorder.

Nonetheless, I suspect that there may be some relationships, although this impression is based on only a few cases so far. One woman who scored very thick was a patient who came to the sleep disorders center complaining of a very unusual kind of insomnia. She had an obsession about sleep; she would lie in bed, thinking over and over, "I can't sleep; I'm never going to sleep again; I'll die of not sleeping." Sometimes she even heard voices inside her head telling her these same things. She met the criteria for the diagnosis of obsessive-compulsive disorder, a relatively rare illness characterized by obsessive thoughts, such as this woman had, or by compulsive, repetitive acts and rituals. (This condition is not the same as obsessive-compulsive personality disorder, although some patients with the illness have had the personality disorder as well.) She obtained some help from a medication used specifically to treat obsessive-compulsive disorder.

Two other cases involved severe alcoholics who

scored very thick on the Boundary Questionnaire. Alcoholism is a complex, multifaceted condition or group of conditions, and I am by no means suggesting that alcoholics in general have thick boundaries; in fact, I have also seen alcoholics who score very thin. But the two I have in mind are part of a definable subgroup of alcoholics who are totally smooth and charming, seem to have a lot of friends (although often the friendships are superficial), and steadfastly deny that they have any problem with alcohol, even when there is evidence to the contrary all around them. Discussions with them about the problem slide off them like water off a duck's back. This particular duck's back, also known as denial, can be seen as one kind of very thick boundary, and in the cases I have in mind it was accompanied by many other thick characteristics, such as seeing the world in blacks and whites and having absolutely solid "us versus them" group boundaries.

So far these few clinical cases provide the only suggestions of mental illnesses related to having thick boundaries.

ADAPTATION TO STRESS

My impression, based on my clinical work with patients who have either very thick or very thin boundaries, is that in general people with thicker boundaries are better at dealing with stress, at least the kinds of stress we all occasionally face. They are more likely to continue to work daily at difficult jobs, even jobs they dislike; they are probably more capable of clearing a building in case of fire or making rapid decisions if a truck is heading for them out of control; they appear to function more effectively during a divorce or after a death, perhaps because it does not "get to them" so much. They are especially good at dealing with such work-related stresses as organizational problems. In fact, I would suggest that people with thick boundaries can be considered better adapted to a tough world full of stress. In wartime they are in their element. On the other hand, I have the impression that they do not enjoy life as much as those with thin boundaries when everything is going smoothly. People with thin boundaries are perhaps better adapted to peace.

What I have said may not hold, however, when the stress is catastrophic—when the situation is out of one's control and there is no way to give the right directions or to continue functioning normally. When someone suddenly finds himself or herself dying or taken hostage or imprisoned in a concentration camp the reactions and behavior may be very different. Under such circumstances people act in unexpected ways; a person who is good at handling most kinds of stress may or may not be able to handle catastrophe; he or she may suddenly collapse or break, like the powerful oak in the wind. By contrast, the gentle artist with thin boundaries may sometimes be able to shift to a different mode and survive catastrophe, perhaps even become a hero.

Of course, one's boundaries do not necessarily remain constant during serious stress. As we saw in chapter 6, ordinary stress, especially if prolonged, may produce a thickening of boundaries, but trauma or catastrophe can tear boundaries and make them thinner.

Those of us who work in the fields of psychiatry or clinical psychology are often accused of emphasizing pathology, of always looking for illness and vulnerability. And as indeed I have done so in this chapter and several others, I must plead guilty but with extenuating circumstances. I have been trying to relate the concept of boundaries, and specifically the Boundary Questionnaire, to existing concepts and measures. So much work already exists on the diagnosis and measurement of mental illness and personality disorder that I cannot help referring to these areas. Much less work has been done on mental health in a positive sense. I therefore want to emphasize that the focus on illness does not lie in the nature of the subject; boundaries can also be seen to relate to a variety of strengths. I will discuss creativity—one kind of strength—in the next chapter. Here I will mention a number of other forms of strength that accompany thick and thin boundaries, some of which have been alluded to briefly.

Thick boundaries are clearly related to solidity in many senses: to organization, goal-directedness, reliability, responsibility, and dependability. This list includes just about all the virtues an employer seeks in a prospective employee. Thick boundaries are also related to tolerance to stress in most situations, as we have seen. And thick boundaries involve perseverance or persistence, the virtue Calvin Coolidge valued above all others:

> Nothing in the world can take the place of persistence. Talent will not; nothing is more common than unsuccessful men with talent. Genius will not; unrewarded genius is almost a proverb. Education will not; the world is full of

educated derelicts. Persistence and determination alone are omnipotent. The slogan: "Press On" has solved and will always solve the problems of the human race. (1933)

Strengths associated with thin boundaries include sensitivity, openness, ability to change, and often creativity. These characteristics are obviously valuable and may be especially important for people in certain careers and professions, for example artists, teachers, and therapists.

Overall I believe that the basic structure of our boundaries is certainly one important factor in the mental and physical problems we develop, and in the way we adapt to the often stressful world around us. The connections between boundaries and resistance to stress, and more generally between boundaries, health, and illness, definitely require further exploration.

WHICH IS BETTER: THICK OR THIN?

It may be worth discussing briefly the question of whether having thick or thin boundaries is better or more adaptive in an overall sense. As I use the concept, and as I examine the data on thin and thick boundaries, I make absolutely no value judgment; I do not consider one end of the continuum better than the other. We have seen that thin boundaries clearly have adaptive aspects—openness, certain creative abilities, and so on—and also maladaptive aspects, such as vulnerability, and the tendency to become lost in fantasy or to be hurt too easily. Thick boundaries are adaptive in making one well organized, punctual, reliable, responsible, and efficient but may be maladaptive insofar as they lead to rigidity and inability to change. Our language reflects these two related aspects of thick boundaries: the verb *persevere* [from the Latin *perseverare,* "to follow through, to continue firmly"] has produced two different English nouns, *perseverance* and *perseveration.* Perseverance is a great virtue; we can think of it as the quintessential thick virtue. But perseveration is an inability to stop what one is doing, to change course even when it is clear that the course one is on is going nowhere or is leading to disaster; in severe forms it can be a symptom of frontal lobe brain damage. It could be considered the thick vice or defect.

It may surprise my readers that I attach no value judgment to thick versus thin boundaries. My conclusion from lectures and discussions about boundaries is that a great many people feel strongly one way or the other; they consider one end of the continuum definitely superior. And my impression is that most people are comfortable with, and prefer, the sort of boundaries they have themselves.

Many people I have spoken with who seem to have thin boundaries themselves (including some in whom this was confirmed on the Boundary Questionnaire) are convinced that thin boundaries are preferable. They emphasize the negative characteristics of people with thick boundaries, finding them rigid, dull, obsessional, "armored." Furthermore, they are certain that I must have thin boundaries, because I am an author or because they consider my work imaginative, and they assume that I too must prefer thin boundaries to thick, even though I am too polite to say so.

On the other hand, people who obviously have thick

boundaries themselves are quite convinced that thick boundaries are superior—that they indicate solidity, reliability, dependability, and normality—while thin boundaries suggest "flakiness," unreliability, and sickness of some kind. And they are sure that I, as a scientist and a physician, must have thick boundaries myself and must prefer thick boundaries, although I don't say so to avoid hurting the feelings of the fragile "thins."

Perhaps it is only to be expected that people who have grown up with or grown up into one boundary style or the other should approve of it or at least feel comfortable with it. As a general rule, people are often dissatisfied with their current state but tend to be satisfied with their own long-term traits (although others may complain of them.)

CHAPTER 10

Boundaries, Creativity, and Madness

Great wits are sure to madness close allied
And thin partitions do their bounds divide
—John Dryden

THERE IS CLEARLY an overlap between certain aspects of thin boundaries and certain aspects of mental illness. A sense of coming apart, an inability to distinguish fantasy from reality, feelings of merging with another person, loss of one's own identity, frightening dreams difficult to shake off when awake—all these can be symptoms of mental illness, especially of schizophrenia and schizophreniform disorder, when they become pervasive and take over one's life. In less severe but chronic form, they can be symptoms of schizotypal personality disorder. In this sense, having thin boundaries sounds like a dangerous condition, a condition close to or predisposing to madness.

At the same time, certain aspects of thin boundaries such as sensitivity, openness, and awareness of one's deepest feelings appear to characterize artists and creative people in general. A number of noted artists are known to have had frequent nightmares and apparently had thin boundaries in many senses. Our nightmare studies found that people with lifelong nightmares and thin boundaries shared several different potentials: in some of the nightmare sufferers one could clearly see a development toward artistic creativity, in others a movement toward psychosis; sometimes both tendencies were present in the same person (Hartmann 1984).

We have seen that the Boundary Questionnaire bears out this two-sided potential of thin boundaries. In the last chapter we noted that patients in our sample with the diagnoses of schizotypal personality disorder, borderline personality disorder, and schizophrenia all scored much higher (thinner) than average, and in chapter 4 we saw that two groups of art students also scored unusually thin.

There is a great deal of disagreement as to whether creativity can be measured, but some scales of creativity have been developed; in one recent study (Levin et al. 1991) the same seventy-nine students took the Boundary Questionnaire and two different measures of creativity: the "Unusual uses of a brick test" (Guilford et al. 1957) and the "Remote associates test" (Mednick 1962). The first simply asks subjects to list as many uses as possible for an ordinary brick. The second test presents subjects with groups of three words (for example "rat, blue, cottage") and asks them to find a fourth word related to all three (in this case "cheese" would be the answer).

The results demonstrated only a trend: There was a weak positive correlation (*r*'s between .10 and .22) between all three measures, but neither the correlations between the Boundary Questionnaire and the creativity measures, nor even the correlation between the two creativity measures reached statistical significance. Thus thin boundaries tended to relate slightly to creativity on these two tests, but the two tests were not measuring the same thing.

Obviously creativity is not unitary or easy to measure. Furthermore, it seems that in terms of boundary structure, being an art student is not the same as producing creative artistic work and becoming recognized for it. Stephanie Beal (1988) found that established artists score quite differently from art students on the Boundary Questionnaire. She studied four groups of established artists—sculptors, composers, instrumentalists, and instrument-makers—most of them between forty and fifty years old at the time of the study. She was especially interested in differences between the "pure creative" artists—the sculptors and composers—and the "interpretive" artists—the instrumentalists and instrument-makers. A total of seventy-two artists in these categories were compared with thirty-six control subjects of roughly the same age, sex, and socioeconomic status.

One important finding was that overall these established artists did not score significantly thinner than the controls; the scores were similar (an adjusted mean SumBound of 283 for the artists and 278 for the controls), and both the artist group and the control group scored not far from our overall average but much thicker than the two groups of art students, even when adjusted for age. When the different categories of artists were examined separately, the pure creative artists did score thinner than the others. The two groups of pure creative artists also differed from each other; the sculptors scored much thinner than the composers. A comparison of their scores on the categories and factors of the Boundary Questionnaire demonstrated that the pure creative artists scored markedly thinner on the categories sleep/dream/waking, unusual experiences, and child-adolescent-adult and on factor I (primary process thinking) and factor III (identification with children). The single question on the Boundary Questionnaire that best separated the pure creative artists from the others was "I spend a lot of time daydreaming, fantasizing, or in reverie."

The difference between the groups of established artists and the art students is intriguing. Clearly the established artists score much thicker. We cannot be certain whether the recognized artists represent the subgroup of art students who had some thick characteristics all along—in other words, those who would not have scored very thin even while they were art students—or whether they had been typical thin-scoring art students who later built up more solid boundaries (defenses, perhaps) and thus scored thicker only because they took the questionnaire in their forties or fifties. Clearly the relationship between boundaries and artistic creativity is not a simple one. My interpretation, based not only on these data but on clinical work with artists, is that becoming a recognized artist certainly requires sensitivity and openness as well as artistic talent but that in addition some thicker qualities, such as perseverance and perhaps business and organization skills, are involved in completing one's work and getting it before the public.

Of course even the creation of a work of art usually involves more than pure inspiration or openness to new ideas. It requires not just combining elements in a new way, condensing, sometimes regressing (and thin boundaries should be helpful here), but also moving forward and building on the inspiration (and some thickness is useful here). Ernst Kris introduced the felicitous phrase "regression in the service of the ego" to describe artistic creation (1952, p. 177). The regression may be helped by thinness, but "in the service of the ego" requires that one not be too thin, at least in the sense of fragile or vulnerable, so that one can build something and not fall apart as a result of the regression.

Different arts and different situations may require different mixes of thin and thick. One can imagine, as an extreme case, a painter or lyric poet, inspired by a new vision, dashing off a significant work in the course of a few hours (Picasso and Coleridge come to mind), but it is hard to imagine a composer creating an entire symphony in such a brief time (although Mozart may have come close). In fact composers often benefit from an organizing or structural skill for their work, not to mention the hard work and perseverance needed to master one or more instruments; thus it is not surprising that composers do not score so thin overall on the Boundary Questionnaire. Similarly, an architect designing a cathedral would require a great degree of organization and perseverance, which involve aspects of thick boundaries, in addition to creativity. The stereotype of the romantic artist, living totally for art, unable or unwilling to manage the dull routines of everyday life, certainly fits the very thin boundary type, but actual artists are a bit more complicated.

Overall, then, having thin boundaries is a complex condition that can perhaps lead to artistic interests and involvement but is obviously not sufficient to assure artistic achievement. And having thin boundaries may involve a greater vulnerability to certain kinds of mental illness but cannot be considered a sign of being "sick." It is not difficult to see how certain aspects of thinness, such as sensitivity, openness to one's own feelings and inner states as well as those of others, or a tendency to see, hear, and feel everything very powerfully and vividly (an "inability to keep things out") could lead to turmoil and mental illness but could also be important and useful in a developing artist.

I prefer this explanation to the alternative of proposing two kinds of thin boundaries: a "bad" kind leading to illness and a "good" kind leading to art. We can think of thinness as a personality tendency or predisposition that can sometimes lead in the direction of art or in the direction of madness or both. If this predisposition is recognized in a child or adolescent, one can help by fostering and encouraging specific artistic talents; also specific, dangerously thin boundaries can be identified, discussed, and strengthened in psychotherapy.

MIXTURES OF THICK AND THIN

In the course of this book I have frequently described and discussed people who have very thin or very thick boundaries overall. Most people, however, have either boundaries that fall somewhere in between or a mixture of thick and thin boundaries. In the last section we discussed one kind of mixture of boundaries, noting that successful artists did not have totally thin boundaries; they resembled the art students in some ways, such as a tendency to daydream, but they had developed some thick boundaries as well. We will now examine other sorts of mixtures of thick and thin—people who are not at either end of the continuum.

It is less exciting to discuss a middle range than to look at extremes. Imagining an ordinary, average sort of person whose boundaries are neither very thick nor very thin is easy and perhaps not particularly fruitful. What may be worthwhile, however, is to examine situations where one boundary or group of boundaries is especially thin while others are thick, or vice versa. Such an approach may teach us something about the interaction between boundaries and perhaps help us understand how boundaries are formed and altered.

Given the many types of boundaries described in chapter 2, each of which could be either thick or thin, it is theoretically possible to postulate a huge number of combinations. My experience, however, suggests that the various types of boundaries move together to a great extent and that someone who is very thin in one way tends to be thin in others as well. Similarly, the data from the Boundary Questionnaire indicate a strong correlation between the individual questions, which together are designed to cover the entire range of types of boundaries, and the overall boundary score, SumBound.

Still, things cannot be quite this simple. Clearly there

are clusters or groups of boundaries that are found together more than other possible groupings. The factor analysis of the Boundary Questionnaire (chapter 4; and Harrison et al. to be published) reveals the presence of such groupings or factors and can help us examine the groups of questions that hang together and correlate with each other. By far the strongest grouping is described by factor I, called *primary process thinking,* which indicates experiences of merging or fluctuating identity, vivid imagery difficult to tell from reality, and so on. If we start by examining the correlation of the different subject categories of boundaries on the questionnaire, we find that the strongest grouping involves categories 1, 2, and 3—questions dealing with sleeping/waking/dreaming, unusual experiences, and thoughts, feelings, and moods. And in fact most of the questions in these categories are the ones that make up factor I, so this approach leads basically to the same grouping. The questions that load most strongly on this factor (or can best represent this factor) are "In my daydreams, people kind of merge into one another or one person turns into another" and "I have had the experience of someone calling me or speaking my name and not being sure whether it was really happening or whether I was imagining it." There is no doubt that this sort of inner boundary grouping holds together; it seems likely, therefore, that we should be able to find people who are thin in these ways but not thin in others.

A second very strong grouping emerges from the correlated categories 8, 10, 11, and 12—questions dealing with preferences in edges, lines, and clothing and with opinions about organizations, groups, nations, and beauty and truth. The questions in these categories show up to a great extent on factor II, which we call *preference for explicit boundaries.* The questions that best represent this factor are "I like clear, precise borders," "There is a place for everything, and everything should be in its place," and "A good relationship is one in which everything is clearly defined and spelled out." This grouping could be called outer boundaries or boundaries in the world, because it expresses chiefly preferences and opinions about the outside world. The strength of this grouping suggests that we should be able to identify people who are thick in these ways but not thick in others.

There are no other strong groupings of correlations among the boundary categories, and all the remaining factors include smaller groups of questions and are less reliable. To keep things simple, therefore, let us restrict our discussion to these two major factors and consider what sorts of people might be thin in one way and thick in the other.

First, who is thin inside (factor I) and thick outside (factor II)? Among the preselected groups who took the Boundary Questionnaire, there were four groups that we expected a priori would score thin: two groups of nightmare sufferers and two groups of art students and music students. And so they did, in terms of their overall scores. Three of these four groups scored very thin on both factors I and II. The fourth group, however, made up of conservatory students (graduate music students), scored very thin on factor I but thicker than average on factor II. I do not have additional information on the individual students, so one can only state that as a group these music students apparently had some of the artistic inner thinness we have described but also some thickness in terms of their external preferences and opinions. None of the twenty other groups of students or research subjects demonstrated this particular pattern.

In an effort to understand what this pattern might imply, I searched our overall files for individuals who showed a "thin inside, thick outside" pattern of this kind. Among those who had this pattern in the most extreme degree, ten turned out to be patients with serious psychiatric problems. They had diagnoses of schizophrenia, severe borderline personality disorder, and in a few cases drug or alcohol abuse; some had more than one of these diagnoses. Five of these patients had made suicide attempts.

The records indicate that these were people who had had an early tendency to be thin, with more of the fragility or vulnerability features than most. They had then built up various defensive structures, such as avoidance of potentially painful situations, inhibition of sexual or aggressive feelings, and perhaps isolation of feeling from thought. As adults they apparently wanted their world to be straightforward, well organized, in clear black and white, to protect themselves from feeling pain. Some of these patients had definite paranoid tendencies and diagnoses of either paranoid schizophrenia or other paranoid disorder, and the paranoid mechanisms such as projection can be seen as a tough outer boundary, surrounding and defending a thin inner core. It was striking that there was far more psychopathology (mental illness) in those with this "thin inside, thick outside" pattern than in those who scored thin overall or thick overall.

The group that scored extremely thin inside and thick

outside also included a few art students who were having a difficult time and were developing psychological problems, but not one of the seventy-two successful artists scored in this pattern. Some of the nightmare sufferers presented this pattern of very thin on factor I and relatively thick on factor II. This latter finding was a bit surprising; we had expected nightmare sufferers to score thin on all aspects of boundaries, since the questionnaire was originally based on interviews with nightmare groups. Some indeed did score consistently thin, but the mixed pattern was found in quite a few, and again our impression was that the thick outer boundaries were defensive, probably a protection or defense that resulted when fragile inner boundaries met a tough outside world. In fact, in all the situations we have discussed, it appeared that the thin inner boundaries were primary, or present earlier, and the thick outer boundaries seemed to be defensive or protective and to have developed later.

Some more extreme cases of this process can be seen in people who join cults or people who throw themselves totally into a new cause or group. Such people use the cult or group to strengthen themselves or to replace a vulnerable part of their own egos. The ones I have seen in therapy can certainly be described as having thin inner boundaries and adopting a set of strong outer boundaries to help them feel less vulnerable. In these cases the inner fragility is often quite prominent, and although the outer thick shell is protective, it is often not smooth or comfortable. When the ratio of thick to thin is higher, the result might be a cult leader or a dictator. In such a person the inner thinness or fragility would be extremely well hidden behind massive thick boundaries. This person not only would wear solid, well-fitting armor but would have a very thick skin that reaches deep inside. The cult or cause would then be absorbed and internalized, and the leader could be utterly convincing to others and often to himself.

Some great men and women might be described in this way, but some master criminals and dictators might be included, too. I am thinking of those who "conquer the world" in one way or another as a compensation for some inner hurt or some perceived flaw they must overcome. Obviously the thin-inside-thick-outside combination can potentially be very powerful and also very dangerous, but I have little real data to back up the last few speculations; I do not have long lines of dictators and cult leaders waiting to enter my office or my research laboratory.

What about the opposite combination—thick on factor I but thin on factor II, or thick inside and thin outside? No single group in our studies scored as clearly in this direction as the music students did in the opposite direction, but two groups showed a definite tendency toward the thick inside, thin outside pattern. One group was the "friends of artists," a control group for the successful artists consisting of thirty-six friends who were the same age and sex but were not artists themselves. These men and women, most of them aged forty to sixty, were in most cases successful at something themselves; some were art dealers or art collectors. The other group consisted of fifty graduate or advanced undergraduate students in counseling psychology at a Catholic university, although they were not necessarily Catholic themselves. The scores of these students definitely tended toward the pattern of thick inside but thin outside, far more so than the scores of several other large student groups in our sample.

It is not immediately obvious what these two groups might have in common that would tend to result in this thick inside, thin outside pattern. Again, looking at some individuals who scored in this way might be helpful. Among those whose scores were most extreme for the pattern we are discussing (thick inside, thin outside) was a woman in her forties who was a member of a religious order. She was extremely intelligent, a successful teacher and counselor, and was becoming known as a leader in her order, although it was hard for her to acknowledge her own success. I thought of her as a strong person, but she was not so sure. She had solid ties with her family and appeared to have a definite identification with her father as well as with her mother. She did not have the acute sensitivities or experience the vivid imagery that go with high (thin) scores on factor I. Yet she was definitely thin in most other ways: she preferred loose or open divisions, disliked rigid rules, and saw everything in shades of gray.

The others in our sample who scored in this thick-inside-thin-outside pattern were among the older individuals in our groups; many were in their fifties or sixties. Many were successful professionals—not lawyers, who as we have seen tended to score thick overall, but physicians, psychologists, nurses, and professors. They had little or no psychopathology: very normal MMPI scores and no psychiatric diagnoses on interview. They impressed the interviewers as having considerable inner strength, and in fact all scored above average on a special MMPI scale (Es) measuring ego strength. They were definitely flexible and relativistic in their views; they could be called "solid liberals."

The impression I obtained from those I have seen in therapy is that these people grew up with strong identifications, usually in solid families. They did not have especially vivid dreams or daydreams, nightmares, or acute sensitivities. They were intelligent but not strikingly artistic in childhood and adolescence. I felt that in their teens they might well have scored thick overall on the Boundary Questionnaire but that later their outer boundaries gradually loosened or thinned, perhaps because the world was not overly stressful for them and they found they did not have much need for defense or protection. In this sense they could be said to have become more flexible as they grew older. They and their friends usually saw this as a positive change; they had mellowed, become more open and less tough and rigid. Often the change had happened gradually and spontaneously; in a few cases these were people with obsessive-compulsive features who had undergone a successful psychoanalysis or long-term psychotherapy.

In both types of thin/thick mixtures we have examined, the data suggest that the inner boundaries (measured by factor I) appeared earlier and that the outer boundaries arose, to some extent at least, as a reaction or protection. This idea makes good sense; it would be hard to imagine outer boundaries appearing first. By the age of six or even earlier, a child can certainly have thin or thick boundaries in terms of imagery, dreams, daydreams, thought and feeling, and so on, but firm and lasting preferences and opinions about the world are at most only beginning to develop. Thus it seems likely that the boundaries measured by factor I are not only inner, but also earlier and more basic and that they refer to a structuring of the mind produced by genetic or very early environmental factors. The groups of boundaries measured by factor II are outer and develop later, perhaps as a result of interactions between the already developed inner boundary structure and the outside world.

Among those whose genetics, in combination with their earliest environment, equip them with very thin inner boundaries, several paths are possible. Some, as we have just seen, require defense, a protection around their thin core, and develop thick outer boundaries. Others either do not require this protection, perhaps because their environment is unusually accepting, or are unable to develop thicker outer boundaries; these people remain thin in both senses.

Among those with a thick inner core, some move in the direction of gradually thinning or loosening their outer boundaries. Others have pervasive thick boundaries that never become thinner, perhaps because the boundaries function well and adaptively or perhaps because the boundary structures are so solid that they cannot under any circumstances become thinner; these are the people who maintain totally thick inner and outer boundaries.

PART THREE

PRACTICAL AND THEORETICAL IMPLICATIONS

CHAPTER 11

Applications of Boundaries in Clinical Practice and Research

BY NOW IT SHOULD be clear that I believe the concept of boundaries in the mind—thin and thick boundaries—can be useful in a number of ways. We have already seen that it is helpful in connecting or unifying very diverse data. It was useful to me in characterizing the people with lifelong nightmares; rather than having to describe these people as somewhat unusual in ten or twenty different ways, I was able to say that they had thin boundaries. We have found relationships between thin or thick boundaries and any number of interesting human characteristics. For example, in the last chapter we examined the possibility that thin boundaries may be a possible link between "genius" and "madness"—between a certain kind of vulnerability to mental illness and an important part of artistic creativity. In practical terms, this link suggests that because thin boundaries appear to be present from early childhood, children with thin boundaries can develop either in the direction of creativity or in the direction of mental illness—or both. Knowing this potential for divergent development may help us nudge them in the healthier direction.

The concept may also be unifying in the sense that a number of the mechanisms of defense, such as repression and isolation, can be seen as different aspects of thick boundaries or the thickening of boundaries. Moreover, if it can be accepted that boundaries have some cohesiveness—that there is a common feature to all the types of boundaries we have discussed—and if, as I suggested at the beginning, the common feature involves separateness versus togetherness or insulation versus connectedness with respect to any two constituents, functions, or processes in the mind, then the concept has a heuristic simplicity that can lead to all sorts of progress, including a link to the biology of the brain.

There are two broad questions, one theoretical and one practical, that will determine whether this way of delineating personality will be useful and enduring. The theoretical question, to be discussed in the next chapter, has two parts: Does this make sense psychologically? (Does it help fill in the psychological map describing what is going on in our heads?) And does it make sense biologically? (Does it relate to the developing biological map of what is going on in these same heads?) The broad practical question is the obvious one: So what? Does it make any difference? If I know I have thin boundaries, or if I know this patient with cancer has especially thick boundaries, or that suicidal patient has thin boundaries in some senses, will it affect my actions? Should I do things any differently?

I believe the concept of thick and thin boundaries can be, and has already been, useful in a number of practical clinical senses. For some people, simply describing themselves in a new way seemed to be helpful. A number of people—not only patients in psychotherapy but also a number of artists and colleagues—told me they found the realization "I have really thin boundaries" both useful and reassuring. It was useful because it seemed to fit them so well and to describe things about themselves they had not quite known how to characterize or explain. And it was reassuring because they felt more understood and less alone. Some felt they could use the concept to relate to artistic people and to artistic parts of themselves, instead of thinking of themselves as strange and idiosyncratic. For many people, especially adolescents, being different from others is very frightening and means being "sick." Becoming aware of their boundary structure, recognizing its adaptive as well as its problematic aspects, and seeing themselves as part of a continuum was very reassuring to a number of them.

For patients in psychotherapy, the new perspective and the comfort of feeling less alone often led to further progress, in several different ways. Some patients could accept that thin boundaries were part of their makeup and would try to notice and make use of half-hidden creativity, or a talent for empathy, or a talent for teaching. Others could decide which boundaries needed work and might be changed: "I like my thin boundaries in most ways; my sensitivity is something I would never want to lose. But I'm beginning to see that I can't go through life trusting everyone totally and getting hurt the way I've been doing." For patients at the other end of the continuum, the idea of thick boundaries sometimes helped them articulate and work on their sense of being "walled in," "in a rut," or "not in touch."

Of course such realizations occur anyway, regardless of what terms one uses to describe oneself. *Boundaries* is just a way of conceptualizing information, just a new word. Yet words are important. Three different psychotherapists told me that using the words *thin boundaries* with a number of their patients had greatly facilitated the patients' progress. The specific problem they described was that when patients learned, from insurance forms or some other source, that their official diagnosis was "borderline personality disorder" or "schizotypal personality disorder," they would want to discuss and understand these terms. The discussions were always very difficult, however, because the patients would feel criticized rather than understood by descriptions such as "characterized by unstable relationships," "use of devaluation or manipulation," and "lack of control of anger." The therapists reported that when they introduced the concept of boundaries—"It seems to me that you have extremely thin boundaries in a number of ways"—the patients had a sort of "A-ha experience," agreed that the description fitted them well, and were able to discuss it and use it to make progress.

A knowledge of boundaries can be useful in prediction and sometimes in prevention of psychopathology. As we saw in chapter 9, certain types of pathology are closely related to boundary structure: schizotypal personality disorder may develop in people who have very thin boundaries and presumably have had them since childhood; obsessive-compulsive personality disorder may develop in those with very thick boundaries. In some cases, therefore, thinking about a patient's boundary structure in childhood and adolescence can help the clinician detect early signs of these personality disorders and help prevent the development of the disorders, or at least reduce their severity.

The usefulness of the boundary concept is not limited to individual therapy. As we have discussed, boundary structure plays an important part in relationships and certainly a discussion of boundaries can be useful in couples therapy and in marital therapy. In fact, as we noted in chapter 3, family therapy is one area in which boundaries—at least interpersonal boundaries—are already an important part of the discussions and formulations. The Boundary Questionnaire could quite possibly provide useful information in all these settings.

Knowledge of boundaries can also be helpful in the medical and psychological treatment of many conditions that may themselves have little or nothing to do with boundaries. We have already discussed in some detail in chapter 8 the data gathered on patients suffering from insomnia. We concluded that insomnia is found in people with all kinds of boundaries, but that the different sorts of insomnia reflect different boundary structures and require very different treatments. Serious depression is another common condition that is found in people with all kinds of boundaries but that may take different forms depending on the patient's boundary structure. In my experience certain kinds of guilt often found in depression—the sense that one is responsible for all the problems of others, or taking onto oneself all the troubles of the world—are characteristic of people with thin boundaries. Again, this understanding can be a helpful guide when one is choosing among the many treatment modalities used for depression.

I believe boundary structure may have a powerful influence on the symptom picture, and thus on treatment strategy, in any number of purely medical illnesses. Two patients may have very similar cancers in terms of tissue type, size, and location, and yet their overall illness—how sick they feel, what symptoms they develop—will vary depending on a number of factors such as the psychological defenses they use, whether they adapt to the cancer and change their lives or "fight it all the way," and so on. These factors, which depend to a great extent on the patient's boundaries, are important in planning overall treatment and management.

Some specific treatments may depend even more directly on boundaries. For example, there is great interest in whether mental imagery techniques may be able to help the body fight cancer and other related illnesses (reviewed in Sheikh and Kunzendorf 1984; Kunzendorf and Sheikh 1990). In a study to be described in the next chapter, we found that people with thin boundaries produce more change in their skin temperatures when imagining a warm or a cold situation than do people with thick boundaries. And we have seen that the amount and vividness of imagery in general are related to thin boundaries. It therefore seems likely that such imagery techniques, if they do work, would work far better in people with thin boundaries. It is possible that they are effective *only* when there is a certain degree of boundary thinness. Here knowledge of boundaries could help in choosing patients who might benefit from such treatments.

In addition, research studies investigating these and other techniques could benefit from a knowledge of the boundary structure of the research subjects. A treatment involving imagery might look ineffective—no more effective than a control treatment or no treatment—when studied in an average mixed population or a population that happened to include a number of patients with thick boundaries. But the same treatment might show significant effects if studied in a group of patients most likely to be able to use it—those with thin boundaries. Similarly, hypnosis and relaxation techniques are in use or under investigation in the treatment of hypertension, headaches, chronic pain, and other conditions (reviewed in Brown and Fromm 1987). These techniques often depend on the hypnotizability or suggestibility of patients using them, and hypnotizability, as we have seen, is correlated with thinness of boundaries.

In fact, I believe that knowledge of boundary characteristics can be important when evaluating the effect of almost any drug or medication. People with thin boundaries tend to be sensitive in many ways, including their reactions to chemical substances. In our studies of 900 people who took the Boundary Questionnaire, we found a clear positive correlation between overall boundary score (thinness) and reports of having had unusual reactions to alcohol, marijuana, and coffee or tea, all three of highly significant levels ($p < .001$). In the testing of a new medication, therefore, when it is essential to detect any reactions or side effects, it would be important to use a test population consisting of, or at least including, people with thin boundaries. On the other hand there are research situations in which one might want to avoid unusual reactions or side effects. In a study comparing two different medications whose side effects are already established, one might want to choose groups unlikely to show unusual reactions or side effects that might make interpretation of the results difficult, especially if relatively small groups of patients were being studied. Here it might be advantageous to use patients with relatively thick boundaries.

CAREER CHOICES

People usually choose careers or jobs that somehow seem to suit them, and careers and occupations have a way of choosing people who fit. People who do not fit are sometimes kept out by entrance exams of some kind, or are dropped early in their careers, or just become increasingly unhappy with the "wrong job" and finally quit. Many factors are involved, but I believe one's thin or thick boundaries are among the important variables determining a successful or comfortable choice of career.

Some of the relevant characteristics are obvious. Certain jobs—accountant, librarian, lawyer, engineer, military officer—require an ability to be highly organized and to appreciate tight organization. A person considering these occupations must have thick boundaries at least in these senses. That does not necessarily mean that to be a good librarian one must have very thick boundaries overall; in fact, I know some excellent librarians who feel comfortable with thick boundaries in their work yet have thinner boundaries in other respects.

Among the groups I have studied, there were several professions whose members scored especially thick on the Boundary Questionnaire. One such group was the line naval officers. It makes sense that a military career would appeal to and be comfortable for someone who is not only well organized, as an accountant or librarian would have to be, but who also has a strong sense of hierarchical organization—is able to give and take orders—and a solid sense of group membership—is able to identify strongly with a particular unit, a branch of service, and the nation. Not coincidentally, the military prides itself on *being* a thick boundary, a protective shield or armor against the nation's enemies.

Salespeople (who in our sample were mostly men) also seemed to have thick boundaries. To some extent order and organization are important in sales, but my guess is that other factors are even more important. We have already discussed the tendency to categorize, which may work better in sales than in many other fields. There is also the tendency to think in blacks and whites, rather than shades of gray. Salespeople must be able to convince buyers, and preferably themselves as well, that their products are superior to the competition's products. And salespeople must be well armored in the sense of being able to tolerate rejection. A salesperson may be turned down 90 percent of the time, yet have to bounce back and try again. Someone with thin boundaries would find it difficult if not impossible to continue without feeling hurt and rejected.

Lawyers and businesspeople in the samples I studied, especially middle managers in large organizations, also tended to be people with thick boundaries. Again the sense of order and hierarchy is obviously important here, as well as the tendency to be a solid group member, a "team player."

Those with thin boundaries are often drawn to occupations that do not require strict schedules and detailed organization. As we have seen, the group that scored quite thin on the Boundary Questionnaire included painters, musicians, and writers. Some (but by no means all) teachers, counselors, and therapists also scored quite thin. In all these fields, sensitivity and an openness to one's own inner life as well as to other people are extremely useful. Of course, totally thin boundaries can make working in any field difficult. A certain amount of scheduling, organization, and business sense are always needed; an otherwise fine teacher who cannot get to classes on time or a therapist who misses too many appointments will not last long.

Even artists cannot get along purely on introspection and creative ideas. They usually need some form of thicker boundary to get their work into shape and other kinds of boundaries to get it published, organize a show, obtain grants, and so on. As we have seen, art students scored extremely thin on the Boundary Questionnaire, but the successful artists scored much less thin. Moreover, having really thin boundaries can be painful, even for an artist. I can think of two young artists, both considered unusually creative and innovative and both extremely sensitive, open, and trusting, who became overwhelmed in their early twenties. Both had severe nightmares, became almost psychotic (suicidal in one case), and then developed thicker boundaries but in awkward ways. Percy, mentioned in chapter 6, became a somewhat paranoid loner. The other artist has developed quirks and mannerisms, not avoiding people but making them adapt to her schedule and her whims if they want to be with her; one could say she is developing into an eccentric. Both are continuing their artistic work, but they seem to have slowed down a bit. My impression is that they do not shine as brilliantly among their peers as they did a few years ago.

Scientists need a certain degree of solidity, organization, maybe even compulsivity to carry out their work and to get through the years of necessary training. But they also need an edge of creativity and flexibility, a willingness to leave the established paths and try something new. In this sense they must have some thin as well as some thick boundaries or an ability to switch from one to the other. Great scientists often emphasize the intuition involved in their discoveries, the sense of things flowing together, and the sheer "beauty of the equations." My answer to people asking me how to do scientific work is, "How to do science? First know everything. Then do poetry!"

The distinctions I have described do not mean that people with thick boundaries go off to one type of job or field, while the thin ones go off in another direction, with no meeting between the two. Fortunately society has room for variety and for cooperation. Artists and arts organizations use business managers and agents; a whole profession or group of professions known as arts management has grown up for people who have relatively thick boundaries yet want to be involved in the arts. The business world also has room for both thick-boundary and thin-boundary people. A company may be started by an inventor or innovator, someone with relatively thin boundaries who invents a new product or devises a new way of doing things. Once the business gets going, it may be better managed by people with thicker boundaries, but when it becomes a really large business, it will again need people with thinner boundaries, to work in areas such as the development of new designs, aspects of computer programming, writing, and artwork.

In general, then, people with thick boundaries are usually happier in jobs that are well structured, with clear lines of responsibility, whereas people with thin boundaries are better satisfied in looser, less well-structured settings. But this is far from invariably the case; some people need a job that balances their inner tendencies. One very creative writer and therapist, who in fact scored extremely thin on the Boundary Questionnaire, remembers with great fondness the two years he spent in the army. He feels that the discipline and regimentation of the army, so different from the turmoil of his inner life, were exactly what he needed at the time.

One woman came to see me specifically because she had read my book on nightmares, in which I first discussed thin boundaries. She had nightmares herself, and she wanted to tell me how perfectly the description of thin boundaries fitted her. In fact, she described some kinds of intense sensitivity that I had not heard of before. When I asked about her occupation, she laughed and said, "You won't believe this. I'm a real estate agent, and quite successful." She knew from my book and from talking with me what I would expect in terms of occupations that would go with thin boundaries. And in fact she agreed with me and told me that she herself had done artistic work of several kinds but had found she could not support herself in this way. When someone suggested she try real estate, she first thought it would be totally wrong for her, but it proved to work out very well: "I'm not much good at the business side of it, but I'm great at intuition. I sense very quickly what house will be just right for a particular buyer; I take her right to it, and she's amazed—it's exactly what she's been looking for all these months!"

Of course one does not simply take inventory of one's boundaries and other personal characteristics and jump into a career. One may start with certain tendencies or preferences but often years of education and training intervene, during which one acquires more of a sense of where one fits in, what feels right, and so on. There is a gradual selection of a career by the individual, a simultaneous selection of the individual by the career, and sometimes a process of mutual adaptation. Boundaries play a definite role in this long process of selection and adaptation. An educational or training experience that emphasizes systematic organization of a great deal of material—for example, law school or schools of engineering or other applied sciences—tends to select people with thick boundaries. Training or education that involves shifts of focus and novel approaches—for example acting, theoretical mathematics, philosophy, and perhaps language, in the sense of learning to speak a foreign language as native speakers do—may select for thinner boundaries.

These are only the simplest aspects of the mutual selection process. Obviously the relationships are complex and involve far more than simple thickness or thinness of boundaries. For instance, the data suggest that people with one of the mixtures we have discussed—people who score thick inside but thin outside—function well in a number of different careers including teaching, science, business, and the helping professions.

It will be interesting in the future to relate career choice, career satisfaction, and career success not only with overall thickness or thinness (SumBound) but with the individual factors of the Boundary Questionnaire as well.

CHAPTER 12

Boundaries in the Mind and Boundaries in the Brain

THE POTENTIAL USEFULNESS of the concept of boundaries as a theoretical tool can be explored in two different areas. We can consider it as a psychological concept and look for a link with other ways of describing the mind: Does the concept of thick and thin boundaries help fill in our mental map? Does it help make better sense of data on individual differences and personality structure? In addition, we can look for a link with the biology of the brain. If people with thin boundaries are really different psychologically from people with thick boundaries, can we demonstrate corresponding differences in the structure or functioning of their brains?

Much of the material in the previous chapters speaks to the psychological issue. Before going on to the biology of boundaries, let us consider what has been said about boundaries as a psychological concept.

BOUNDARIES AND OTHER PSYCHOLOGICAL CONCEPTS

I believe that thick and thin boundaries represent a broad personality dimension that encompasses a number of measures heretofore studied separately, including fantasy-proneness, tendency to experience synesthesia, hypnotizability, absorption, tendency to recall dreams, openness, self-disclosure, schizotypy, and aspects of creativity, as well as orderliness, organization, stick-to-itiveness or perseverance, perseveration, and rigidity. Of course this list is an oversimplification. Most of these specific measures can themselves be further analyzed and shown to consist of several factors, so that the concept of boundaries is unlikely to encompass them entirely. It might be more accurate to say that the concept of boundaries captures an important aspect of each of these measures and of many others.

All the measures I have listed are important parts of the mental map, yet they do not fit neatly into the major, relatively well-established personality factors, usually thought to consist of introversion-extroversion and two to four other factors with names that vary according to the theorist (Eysenck 1976; Norman 1963; Cloninger 1986, 1987). Nor does the broad measure of thin versus thick boundaries correspond with any of the personality scales or measures discussed in chapter 5 or to any of the major factors of personality, although not all relationships have been adequately studied.* Thus boundaries

*Detailed examination of the questions and very preliminary studies using small numbers of subjects suggest no close correlations with Eysenck's, Norman's or Cloninger's factors, with the possible exception of a weak positive correlation of thin boundaries with Eysenck's "psychoticism," and with Cloninger's "novelty-seeking."

appear to represent a relatively new, or at least neglected, aspect of personality—an addition to the mental map.

Of course there is still the question whether boundaries should be seen as one broad dimension of personality, as I have suggested, or rather as a number of separate and not necessarily closely related measures or functions. There is something to be said for both positions, and it might even be possible to accept both for different purposes. Certainly one can discuss and study synesthesia or fantasy-proneness or the defenses of isolation and repression or interpersonal barriers in their own right, whether or not there are any relationships among them. And from the psychometric standpoint, results of the factor analysis of the Boundary Questionnaire, which produced a number of orthogonal factors, demonstrate that a number of technically independent dimensions (factors) are being measured by the questionnaire. (My statistical consultants tell me, however, that orthogonal factors inevitably emerge in a questionnaire covering broad content areas and that this by no means suggests one should abandon the overall concept and discuss only the parts.) In any case the statistical analysis can deal only with the structure of this particular questionnaire, which is just one attempt to measure the concept of thick and thin boundaries.

Overall I believe that although the individual types of boundaries are interesting in themselves, the broad concept does hold together. A number of our research findings support this view. First of all, the original group of people with frequent nightmares appeared to have thin boundaries in all senses. That impression was confirmed when two new groups with nightmares took the Boundary Questionnaire; most had thin boundaries in all senses. A group of art students (in painting and sculpture) also had thin boundaries in all senses on the Boundary Questionnaire, whereas a group of naval officers and a number of patients with obsessive-compulsive personality disorder scored thick on all or almost all aspects of the Boundary Questionnaire. High-frequency dream recallers scored significantly thinner than nondreamers, not only on the total boundary score (SumBound) but on each of the twelve content categories of the Boundary Questionnaire. Also compelling are the comments of about fifteen people—patients or colleagues—who had read about the concept of boundaries and who told me that "thin boundaries in all senses" was a perfect description of themselves or of a patient they were treating. If biological studies show differences in brain organization between people who overall score thick and thin—and as we will see shortly, they are beginning to do so—these will provide additional support for the meaningfulness of the concept.

My conclusion is that without question there are identifiable types of boundaries and identifiable factors in the Boundary Questionnaire and that in certain contexts it may be useful to examine these separately. In fact, we have examined mixtures of thick and thin boundaries in chapter 10. But it does not make sense, in my view, to neglect or throw out the broad global view of thick and thin boundaries.

THE BIOLOGY OF BOUNDARIES

I believe that psychology is a higher-order biology, a shorthand description of events in the forebrain (Hartmann 1973, 1982). Any solid psychological description must be describing something in the brain. And I consider this equally true whether the psychological description has been developed by behavioral psychology (such as the concepts of classical [Pavlovian] or operant [Skinnerian] conditioning), by psychoanalysis (such as the defense mechanisms), by descriptive psychiatry (such as the concept of schizophrenia or a "group of schizophrenias"), or by cognitive psychology (such as "modular systems for information processing)."

For me there is no question that if thin and thick boundaries are meaningful psychological terms—if they describe real differences among people in the functioning of the mind—they must also describe real differences in the organization and functioning of the brain. I am aware that not everyone would endorse this statement; there is less than universal agreement on the nature of the relationship between mind and brain. I cannot do justice to the various controversies here, but I will attempt to review briefly some salient features of various attempts to study and relate the fields of psychology and biology. And on the basis of a number of preliminary research findings, I will propose that thin and thick boundaries may refer not only to the mind but to the brain.

Hippocrates wrote, "From the brain and from the brain alone arise all our pleasures, joys, laughter and jests, as well as our sorrows, pains, griefs and tears" (*The*

Sacred Disease, XVII). It has been obvious since antiquity that those things that make us ourselves—our thoughts, memories, plans, wishes, emotions—all basically come from inside our heads. When we say that someone has "heart" or has "guts," we are not referring to that wonderful, durable pump in the chest or the long absorptive tube in the abdomen, but to something about the organization of the marvelously complex organ or group of organs in the head.

Yet this poor head of ours has been the object of study of so many schools of thought in so many disciplines that it must be hopelessly spinning. In the last century or so, the philosophical disciplines have been relatively silent, leaving the study of the head to the various schools of psychology and of biology (neurophysiology, neurobiology, and neurology). The schools of psychology have generally started with large concepts of obvious importance, such as perception, behavior, neurotic symptoms, and language and have developed rapidly when an appropriate technique of study was developed, such as introspection, conditioning experiments, free association, and computer modeling. Each approach has provided valuable insights and information, although these have often been obscured by the dust of battle as each warring camp claimed the entire field as its own.

By contrast, the biological disciplines have begun not with large concepts but with what could be seen: seen first with the eye, then with the microscope, and then with the aid of a rapidly increasing array of instruments and techniques aimed at specific details of nervous system structure and function. Steady progress is being made along many biological fronts; for example, there is already a fairly respectable mammalian biology of sensation and motor functioning (the periphery of the nervous system). For the most important central psychological concepts, however, there is barely the beginning of a biology.

Both sets of disciplines are attacking the same basic issues—what is going on inside our heads—yet the approaches of psychology and biology have been so disparate that often there appears to be no dialogue whatever. One problem has been the insistence of some psychologists that their discipline bears no relationship whatever to the brain. I do not think this is a tenable position in the long run, although in the short term it can be important to say, "We just don't know enough about the biology or neurology underlying such-and-such, so let's leave biology aside for now and see how far we can get on a purely psychological level." This in fact was the position taken by Freud ([1898] 1954), who was trained as a neurologist and who developed his theories in psychological terms but always hoped that his psychoanalytic findings would be supported by biology.

A number of links are now being forged between psychology and biology, precisely in places where psychology has provided a clear-cut concept or description for which the biology can be investigated. In the case of classical (Pavlovian) conditioning, for example, or the even simpler learning mechanism known as habituation to a repetitive stimulus, it has long been clear that the biology underlying this sort of learning must involve alterations in the central neurons connecting the sensory input (unconditional or conditional stimulus) and the motor output (response). In recent years, working with a giant snail whose nervous system contains a relatively small number of neurons, Eric Kandel and his associates have elucidated not only the cellular mechanisms but even the molecular mechanisms—changes in ion flow through cell membranes—that underline these simple aspects of learning (reviewed in Kandel 1984). It is not certain, of course, whether these same mechanisms will turn out to underlie learning in other species.

Starting at a very different point, the careful clinical delineation of mental illnesses has led to greatly increased knowledge of the neurological, physiological, and neurochemical aspects of certain relatively well-defined major mental illnesses, such as the depressions and the schizophrenias. Many gaps remain, but we are beginning to understand at least some basic aspects of the biology of these two serious conditions or groups of conditions, which have previously been considered only in terms of their psychological characteristics.

Starting from still a different place, one that has been of great interest to me, we are making progress in understanding the biology underlying the very different mental functioning occurring in dreaming as opposed to waking. Here are two quite different forms of consciousness, following different rules, yet both produced by the same human head. I suggested some years ago (Hartmann 1973), on the basis of a great deal of indirect evidence, that REM sleep, during which most though not all dreaming occurs, was characterized by absence of norepinephrine and perhaps other biogenic amines at the cortex and that this lack accounted for the specific characteristics of dreaming that differentiated it from waking. Studies involving direct recordings of single neurons in the brainstem of cats have now confirmed that during REM sleep the neurons that release norepinephrine at the cortex are indeed almost completely turned off (Aston-Jones and Bloom 1981; Hobson et al. 1983). Here again there is a rapidly expanding biology underlying a psychological state. And I consider some of the psychological descriptions of mental functioning during dreaming, such as Freud's terms *condensation* and *symbolization,* as shorthand descriptions of the way the cerebral cortex functions without the influence of these biogenic amines (Hartmann 1973, 1976, 1982).

These are all places, or psychological regions, in which relatively well-defined and useful psychological terms turn out to refer to a complex underlying brain biology, which we are beginning to understand. The psychological region of most importance to our discussion here is personality. So far there is very little knowledge of the central biology of personality, though as I have argued, such a biology must exist. A few beginnings have been made in this direction, however. For example, research establishing the heritability of aspects of personality (Cloninger 1986; and the twin studies we have discussed) implicate genes that presumably must affect central nervous system functioning.

Laurence Siever and his associates (1984, 1989) have been investigating biological characteristics of certain personality disorders. They have demonstrated, for instance, that a difficulty in smooth pursuit eye movements, first discovered in schizophrenic patients by Holzman and associates (1974), occurs with greater than normal frequency in persons with schizotypal personality disorder. This correlation suggests a relationship between the personality disorder and schizophrenia, but it also demonstrates a biological characteristic of people who have only the personality disorder. Similar beginnings have been made with other personality disorders. This work certainly relates to a biology of personality, although as we have noted earlier, the current personality disorders do not constitute entirely well-defined entities, and their relationship to personality dimensions or traits is not always clear.

There are also some hints as to biological correlates of certain personality *dimensions*. Eysenck and his coworkers have performed a number of studies relating the dimension of extroversion-introversion to the functioning of the autonomic nervous system (Eysenck 1967, 1976); in general, people characterized as extroverts show less autonomic nervous system change (alterations in pulse, respiration, and so on) in response to stimulation than do introverts. One particular personality trait, referred to as sensation-seeking, has been linked to "augmenting and reducing" of evoked responses (Zuckerman et al. 1980). Those people who have more of this quality—who are more "sensation-seeking" or more "hungry for stimulation"—are people whose brains tend to reduce (in relative terms) the amount of activity produced at the cortex when the level of stimulation by light, sound, or other sensation is increased. Those characterized as less "sensation-seeking" show a relative increase in cortical activity when stimulation is increased.

These are only the beginnings of a biology of personality, and so far they do not present a very coherent picture. Although every valid personality dimension should presumably refer to something in the organization of the brain, no solid connections have been demonstrated as yet. I believe, however, that thin and thick boundaries in the mind may be a personality dimension for which we could relatively easily find an underlying brain biology. The concept refers broadly to the degree of connection or separation between any two entities, processes, or functions in the mind. Placing my (not always rewarded) faith in the simplicity of nature, I would suggest that these correspond roughly to entities, processes, and functions in the brain. Thus the very simplest hypothesis would be that thin boundaries might refer to greater communication between such entities, processes, or functions, and thick boundaries might refer to greater separation or less communication between them.

We would have to postulate such differences chiefly in the forebrain, especially the cerebral cortex, whose ten or more billion neurons subserve most of the processes we are interested in. And the boundaries we are looking for would be boundaries or connections not between individual neighboring neurons but between cell assemblies of some kind—probably between large distributed neuronal systems.

The rough hypothesis, then, would be that peo[illegible]le with thin boundaries have more communicatio[illegible] or more complex or flexible communication, betwee[illegible]rain systems or brain cell assemblies, than do peo[illegible]e with thick boundaries. Let us leave the hypothe[illegible] in this rough form for a minute and examine wheth[illegible]there are any actual data that might support such a b[illegible]gy of thick and thin boundaries, or boundaries in the brain. Some preliminary data are already available, and further relevant studies are in progress.

First, it seemed to us worthwhile to examine the boundaries between the major brain states underlying waking, sleep, and dreaming. People with thin boundaries seemed to be describing on a subjective level a great many halfway states between waking, sleep, and dreaming: being half-asleep, being in reverie, daydreaming, being unsure whether they are really awake, and so on; one might be able to examine physiological records of waking, NonREM sleep, and REM sleep to look for in-between or indefinite states. So far we have not conducted a systematic controlled study, but we had a number of all-night sleep records (called polysomnograms), which had been obtained for various reasons on some of the people who scored very thick or very thin on the Boundary Questionnaire. Examining twenty of these records in detail, but not on a totally blind basis, one experienced scorer found far more hard-to-score or indefinite epochs (sections he considered difficult to score definitely as waking, REM sleep, or NonREM sleep, using standard scoring criteria) in the records of the subjects with thin boundaries. We are currently trying to repeat this study, using several independent scorers who are scoring the records on a totally blind basis according to defined criteria for hard-to-score or indefinite epochs; later we hope to specify such criteria for computer scoring and repeat the study on more systematically obtained data. So far there is at least a suggestion that those who have thin boundaries and subjectively report states that are less separated or demarcated also have less-well-demarcated states on their polygraphic records, and conversely those who subjectively report clear-cut divisions have clear-cut divisions in their records.

Robert Watson has done an important study relating thin and thick psychological boundaries to the boundaries between REM and NonREM sleep (1985). He studied "phasic integrated potentials" (PIPs), which are sharp spikes recorded from eye-muscles in humans or animals. In animal studies PIPs can be shown to be very closely associated with the basic phasic brain activity during REM sleep, known as ponto-geniculo-occipital (PGO) spikes (Metz et al. 1975). PGO spikes can be recorded only from electrodes in the brain, so they cannot be recorded in humans, but PIPs, recorded from electrodes placed on the skin near the eye muscles, can give a good approximation of these basic REM events.

PIPs are found almost entirely within REM sleep, but a few are recorded outside of REM, in NonREM sleep. In fourteen adults, Watson found a strong positive correlation of $r = .52$ ($p < .01$) between number of PIPs recorded outside of REM sleep and thinness of boundaries.* In other words, people with thinner psychological boundaries had more of these basic brain spikes outside of their usual location in REM sleep; the boundary between REM sleep and NonREM sleep was more permeable in this sense.

My associates and I recently conducted a small-scale

*Watson did not have our Boundary Questionnaire available at the time of his study; he used the Rorschach measure of thin boundaries we developed to study our original groups of nightmare sufferers, described in chapter 1, which was consistent with the Boundary Questionnaire in finding extremely thin boundaries in people with frequent nightmares.

study examining a very different biological boundary, the boundary between fantasy or imagery and actual skin temperature. (Skin temperature depends chiefly on peripheral blood flow, controlled by the autonomic nervous system, which is in turn influenced by the central nervous system.) Subjects sat in a comfortable chair and were asked to imagine they were sitting by a warm fire with one hand near the fire; later they were asked to imagine they were holding an ice cube in that hand. Meanwhile a sensitive thermometer recorded the skin temperature on the back of the hand to the closest 0.01 degree Fahrenheit.

Twenty subjects who scored either very thick or very thin on the Boundary Questionnaire were studied. Subjects who scored thin produced significantly greater change in the skin temperature of their hands compared with thick-scoring subjects. (It was of interest that the temperature changes were not always in the expected direction; some subjects in each group produced changes in the opposite direction, but the changes were greater in those who scored thin.) All subjects were able to visualize the scenes as requested, but apparently the imagery got through to the temperature control systems better in those who were psychologically thin.

Ross Levin has recently demonstrated in a group of seventy-eight students that most (but not all) who scored very thin on the Boundary Questionnaire also showed unusually strong and lasting autonomic arousal—measured by skin conductance—to an arousal-producing stimulus (Levin and Raulin, in press). This finding again suggests that something got through more readily in those with thin boundaries.

We have administered a battery of neuropsychological tests to nine persons who scored very thick on the Boundary Questionnaire and eleven who scored very thin (Garg and Hartmann, to be published). Both groups were about evenly divided between men and women. The tests involved tasks such as visual and verbal memory, several kinds of learning, picture completion, and figure construction, designed to test the functioning of the two hemispheres and the various regions of the cerebral cortex involved in cognitive functions. These tests are generally used to detect damage in various parts of the brain; since we were studying groups of normal people with no brain damage who differed only on a measure of personality, it was considered unlikely by neuropsychologists that we would find any differences. Yet significant differences were found: the thick-boundary subjects showed more evidence of perseveration (continuing on a task or in a strategy when asked to stop or change) and a more systematic approach to constructing figures. The thin-boundary subjects showed more ability to change strategies flexibly and were better at adopting new strategies on a number of tests. This sort of difference is considered to reflect differences in the functioning of the frontal portions of the cerebral cortex.

These neuropsychological results, though preliminary, suggest that there are measurable differences in brain function in people who differ on the psychological measure of thick versus thin boundaries. The differences are consistent with what we would expect: those with thick boundaries are systematic but show less ability to change course; those with thin boundaries are less systematic but more changeable and more adaptable.

Another approach to the central biology of boundaries that has been of considerable interest to me is to investigate a possible chemistry of boundaries. The most relevant chemistry is the chemistry of the brain, especially of the cerebral cortex. Examining it directly is difficult, but there are indirect approaches, such as pharmacological studies; using drugs whose actions on the chemistry of the brain is known, we can explore whether a drug or medication can change one's boundaries. Even this approach is problematic, however, because we do not have a measure of boundaries that is very sensitive to changes over a period of hours or days; the Boundary Questionnaire was designed to study long-term, stable differences between people, and only some of the questions can be used to investigate short-term changes. I have begun to study the issue clinically, however, by taking careful notes over the past five years whenever a patient or subject whose boundary structure I knew described the effects of some substance. In some cases I asked a series of detailed questions about the effects of particular drugs. I have notes on drug effects in over one hundred people by now, but many different drugs and other substances are involved, so I can draw only very tentative conclusions.

Several drugs produced effects, especially in people with thin boundaries, that I interpreted as a temporary thickening of boundaries. These drugs were the stimulants, including amphetamines, methylphenidate (Ritalin), and cocaine, and some of the antidepressants, including protriptyline, amitriptyline, and the monoamine oxidase inhibitors. The boundaries that changed were primarily the inner (factor I) boundaries. Typical comments were "I could hold my thoughts together better," "I felt less pulled apart," "I felt more alert, all set to work on something," "less daydreamy," "more concentrated," "I felt tougher." One woman with very thin boundaries said, "I know the stimulants are bad for me, but the immediate effect is sometimes very useful. Instead of being pulled in ten different directions by ten different thoughts and feelings, I can get myself together and move in one straight line."

The only drugs that I interpreted as producing an effect in the opposite direction were the hallucinogenic or psychedelic drugs, such as LSD. LSD in particular produced reports of synesthesia, vivid imagery, dreamlike states, and many thoughts all at once that are consistent with many detailed studies of LSD effects. (For a review of such studies, see Freedman 1968.) In terms of boundaries, I interpreted these changes as consistent with a temporary thinning of inner boundaries.* One woman who scored very thin on the Boundary Questionnaire said of LSD, "I can see why some people might like this sort of loosening or merging and the vivid images, but it's not for me. I'm too much like that anyway, without drugs." (These effects were all reported by people with thin or midrange boundaries. None of the patients and subjects with very thick boundaries had taken LSD.)

These preliminary results can at best give us only a hint of the brain chemistry underlying boundaries. They do suggest that the biogenic amines (norepinephrine,

*Freedman (1968) in summarizing what is most striking about the LSD experience speaks of "the capacity of the mind to see more than it can tell, to experience more than it can explicate . . . to experience boundless and 'boundaryless' events, from the banal to the profound" (p. 331).

dopamine, and serotonin) are involved, because the drugs which appear to alter boundaries are all thought to act chiefly on the brain systems releasing these amines and on the receptors for the amines.

These three biogenic amines, released by neurons with cell bodies in the brainstem, have a widespread distribution and widespread effects on the forebrain, including the cerebral cortex. Each acts on several different types of receptors, producing a complex and only partly understood picture that I cannot begin to discuss here. (For a review, see Cooper et al. 1986.) For many reasons I believe norepinephrine and serotonin may be especially important. I would suggest that increasing the overall activity of these two amines at the cortex, which in a rough sense produces a situation similar to that of alert wakefulness, is associated with a relative thickening of boundaries, whereas reducing their activity, which produces a situation more similar to that of REM sleep, is associated with a relative thinning of boundaries.

Along these lines, I would suggest that the chemistry involved in forming or maintaining thick or thin boundaries during growth and development in different individuals may also relate to differences in the activity of these biogenic amines and their long-term effects in modulating cortical activity or organizing cortical processing.

There is little agreement on how best to describe the action of these amines at the cortex. They appear not to be neurotransmitters themselves but to regulate or modulate brain systems depending on other neurotransmitters. I have discussed elsewhere conceptualizations of the functions of norepinephrine as increasing the signal-to-noise ratio, inhibitory sharpening, and increasing focused attention (Hartmann 1973). In the present context, increased signal-to-noise ratio, inhibitory sharpening, and increased focused attention are all terms that could be applied to aspects of thick boundary functioning.

All these results, though very preliminary, support the hypothesis that people who have thin boundaries in our psychological senses also have thin boundaries in some biological senses: they have less distinct boundaries between basic biological states such as waking, NonRem sleep, and REM sleep; their brain activity, measured by PIPs, crosses "boundaries" to appear in unusual places; and they have less of a boundary between the autonomic nervous system and other parts of the nervous system. In terms of their higher cognitive functions, neuropsychological tests indicate that they are more able to let in new information to alter their course. Conversely, those with thick psychological boundaries have more solid biological boundaries in the above biological senses, and the tests suggest that they process material and move forward in straight lines, showing less tendency to let new material change their path. Insofar as brief neurochemical changes can affect boundaries, the changes simulating alert wakefulness with its relatively focused straight-line thinking are felt as a thickening of boundaries, whereas chemical changes simulating REM sleep, associated with dreaming, seem to produce thinning.

All this is consistent with our rough hypothesis that the brain biology of thin and thick boundaries involves something like more complex or multiple connections in the cortex (for thin boundaries) versus relatively simple, straightforward or specific connections (for thick boundaries). We can speak only in a relative sense, however, not of true connectedness versus separateness. Everything in the brain is connected with everything else; it is a truism in neuroanatomy that one can travel from any one spot to any other through at most three or four neurons. But perhaps in some brains the journey can be made in more ways or more different ways or more changeable ways, whereas other brains might have fewer paths, perhaps one or two preferred paths that are used all the time.

Although this book is not the place to discuss details of neuroanatomy or of various models suggested to account for the higher brain functions, it is worth discussing briefly where our boundaries and our more or less flexible connections might be located. Boundaries of some kind occur everywhere in the nervous system; the cell membrane, or boundary around each neuron or nerve cell, is extremely important in the cell's functioning—so important, in fact, that changes in the thickness or permeability of the cell membrane produce far more drastic changes than the individual differences in personality that concern us here. The boundaries we are talking about are almost certainly related to connections between neurons or between groups or assemblies of neurons, perhaps to a variable as simple as the number and strength of synaptic junctions at various places in the cortex.

Assemblies of neurons, also called cell assemblies, exist everywhere in the brain, and perhaps our boundaries too occur throughout the brain. In fact, the tentative data on boundaries between the waking and sleep states suggest that we should not neglect even the brainstem, where these states are principally regulated. A review of all the types of boundaries in the mind described in chapter 2, however—boundaries involving perception, thoughts and feelings, association, memory, preferences, opinions, and so on—leads us inevitably to the forebrain, the cerebral cortex and some underlying structures, which is thought to serve all these complex "higher" functions.

There is a great deal of controversy about how best to understand the workings of the cortex—the ten to fifty billion cells whose one trillion (10^{12}) or more interconnections somehow make possible what we experience, think, feel, are. But however we try to understand it, there must inevitably be individual differences in something that can be called the complexity or flexibility of connectedness. Many theories suggest that the brain—or specifically the cerebral cortex—is or works like a computer. If so, it must be a very unusual computer: it is self-programming, and it has very little hard-wiring (that is, built-in, point-to-point connections). It might make more sense to think of a large number of interconnected computers. For example, whatever it is in our brains that performs mathematical calculations can be thought of as a small, slow computer; whatever finds a name from our memory files for each object that enters our visual field could be another sort of computer. But in this sort of model, the most important—and least understood—aspect is not the insides of the little computers or processing units but the connections between them, the ways they work together. And here there is room for thin and thick boundaries. The connections can be more numerous, more intricate, or more easily alterable in some individuals than in others, or perhaps some people can have more small computers or subsystems working in parallel.

There is evidence that the individual systems or processing units are generally not localized in one place in the cortex, as was previously thought, but are widely distributed. Nonetheless they are obviously connected, and the kind of connection between them is an important variable that allows for differences that can be related to boundaries.

A different model of the brain, one that explicitly rejects the computer analogy, has recently been proposed by Gerald Edelman (1987, 1989). His ingenious model explains the development of perception and eventually other brain functions by a process of "neural Darwinism"—the gradual selection, during development, of certain cells and groups of connected cells according to their fitness for performing perceptual tasks in accordance with a few simple rules. In his model, this process gradually leads to groups of cell assemblies and maps connected by "reentry signalling." Edelman does not refer to differences among individuals, but clearly there must be such differences, related to the amount or richness of the reentry signalling and reentry integration. In Edelman's model I would suggest that those people we have spoken of as having thin boundaries have relatively more, or more complex, reentry connections; people with thick boundaries might be those with fewer or less complex connections—perhaps those in whom the selection process has been especially complete.

I have referred to these models only briefly and very

incompletely to indicate that they allow for differences among individuals in the amount or type of connectivity, which I believe is related to having thick and thin boundaries.

Figure 1 is an oversimplification of what I mean, omitting all the important details of brain organization. In the cortex of a person with thick boundaries, there are relatively straight, specific connections from A to B to C to D. Few detours are taken, and E, F, and G are barely explored. (The letters can represent any sort of cell assembly or distributed neuronal system supporting either a single thought, image, memory, or feeling or a whole group or system of thoughts, images, and so on) The process is fast and straightforward, but not flexible or adaptable. The thin-boundary brain is less restricted to (bounded by) this path. Detours may be taken, the path is longer and less direct, and E, F, and G are explored. D is eventually reached, but so are several other, perhaps

Figure 1

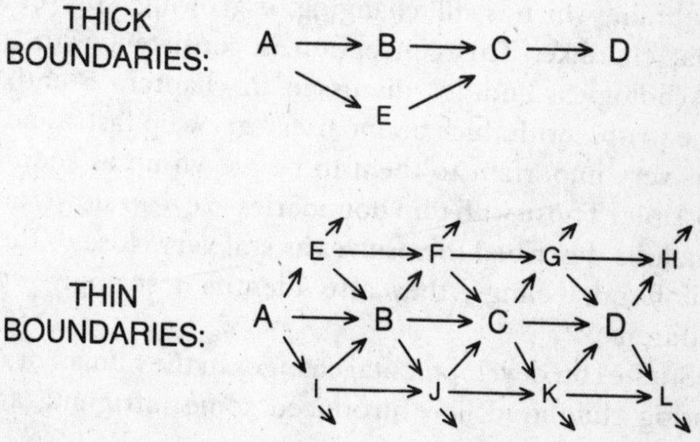

THICK BOUNDARIES: A → B → C → D

THIN BOUNDARIES:

unexpected points, such as H and L. The path is less definite, less specific, less clear, with more branching and more ambiguity. It is a network rather than a single path.

Returning to a computer analogy, one might say that the thick-boundary brain is to a greater extent hard-wired or preprogrammed, whereas the thin-boundary brain is still being programmed or programming itself to a greater extent. This is consistent with my conclusions in past studies of short sleepers, people who regularly require less than six hours of sleep. In chapter 8, the short sleepers were described as "preprogrammed." Reexamining those data convinced me that the short sleepers generally had what we now call thick boundaries. Moreover, we found a significant positive correlation between thickness of boundaries and shortness of sleep in our entire sample of 759 subjects who had reported sleep length on the Boundary Questionnaire.

Looking at the same suggested brain biology in terms of development, one could say that the thick-boundary brain is relatively finished, all grown up, solidified, no longer developing, in comparison with the thin-boundary brain, which is still changing or growing, still somewhat childlike. This conception is consistent with the psychological findings discussed in chapters 5 and 6. The people with thick boundaries "grew up fast," and it was very important to them to be grown up as soon as possible. Those with thin boundaries grew up slowly and as adults described themselves as still very close to their childhood feelings; they also identified strongly with children.

Studies on developmental changes in the human brain during childhood have produced some intriguing and perhaps relevant results. Data from a number of different approaches indicate that there is a clear synaptic pruning—a reduction in the total number of synapses—that occurs somewhere between the ages of five and fifteen. Huttenlocher (1979) obtained this result by direct counting of synapses in postmortem brain samples. Jernigan and Tallal (1990) have shown volume reductions in cortex between the ages of five to fifteen using magnetic resonance imaging (MRI), and Chugani and colleagues (1987) have reported a decline over the same years in cerebral glucose utilization—a measure of brain activity—using positron emission tomography (PET). Feinberg and associates (1982–83, 1989) reported similar changes in the amplitude of delta waves during sleep—another possible measure of cortical activity—and have also demonstrated that very similar statistical models (curves) described all these different changes over time (Feinberg et al. 1990).

All these data suggest that during late childhood—the latency years—the maturing brain reduces the total number of connections (synapses) in the cortex. These are the years we have spoken of previously as the time when boundaries typically solidify or thicken. I would suggest that those in whom this psychological process goes further or is more complete—those with thick boundaries—may be those in whom the process of synaptic reduction or pruning goes further or is more complete. No studies have yet attempted to examine this relationship directly.

The last few pages have admittedly been speculative. A great deal of research needs to be done beyond the very preliminary work described in this chapter. But I hope I have demonstrated that the concept of thin and thick boundaries constitutes an exciting new way to look at personality, that it is a useful addition to our developing map of the mind, and that it may also refer to the organization of our brains. If so, I am happy to have helped a little in following the Delphic injunction *γνωθι σεαυτον*—to know ourselves.

I hope that for the reader who has traveled with me on this journey along the boundaries in our minds, the concept of thick and thin boundaries makes sense as an important and neglected aspect of personality. I believe the concept has implications far beyond the ordinary use of the word *personality* to entail traits such as "she's outgoing" or "he's shy and worries a lot." The concept of boundaries deals with differences between individuals at the most basic levels—differences in the structure of our minds and brains. Such differences, as we are beginning to see, underlie how we learn, think, and remember; how we react to chemicals and how we react to other people; what physical and mental illnesses we may develop; and how we adapt to stress and remain healthy. It is only by understanding such basic differences in the way we are built that we can understand the building blocks and the building itself.

APPENDIX

THIS APPENDIX PRESENTS further data on the Boundary Questionnaire from a more detailed paper (Harrison, Hartmann, and Bevis. The Hartmann boundary questionnaire: A measure of thin and thick boundaries, to be published).

Table A-1 Means (and Standard Deviations) of a Priori Thin and Thick Groups on Boundary Scores[a,b,c]

	A Priori Thin Groups				A Priori Thick-	t Ratios	
	StudyNightmare (N = 17)	*Nightmare (by mail) (N = 12)*	*Museum-sch (N = 20)*	*Music-sch (N = 18)*	*Naval Officers (N = 18)*	*Uncorrected*	*Corrected for Age and Gender*
Personal Total	213 (39)	247 (49)	237 (33)	219 (36)	158 (35)	7.30***	5.24***
World Total	105 (13)	111 (18)	113 (12)	98 (14)	90 (13)	4.59***	3.80***
SumBound	318 (43)	358 (59)	350 (40)	317 (44)	248 (45)	6.97***	5.48***
Pri-Pro	+65 (120)	+105 (111)	+89 (88)	+87 (97)	−32 (57)	4.55***	3.78***
No-Explicit	−24 (78)	+02 (118)	+63 (77)	−35 (118)	−44 (87)	2.35*	ns
Children	−36 (81)	+30 (146)	+28 (91)	−08 (114)	+14 (88)	ns	ns
Fragility	+74 (110)	+51 (117)	+11 (107)	+19 (100)	−69 (116)	3.07**	2.93**
Clairvoyance	+61 (85)	+71 (46)	+17 (104)	−04 (79)	+37 (79)	ns	ns
Openness	−28 (102)	+93 (116)	−11 (104)	+10 (105)	−10 (109)	ns	ns
Planness	+92 (84)	+54 (90)	+45 (68)	+03 (74)	−07 (72)	2.30*	2.47*
Group Bound	−24 (109)	+06 (104)	+40 (88)	+16 (91)	−31 (84)	ns	2.10*
Flexibility	−09 (100)	−12 (60)	+56 (99)	+49 (117)	−77 (75)	3.76***	3.74***

Overinvolv	+11 (141)	−48 (75)	−30 (75)	−25 (95)	−34 (62)	ns	ns
Geometric	+09 (76)	−04 (88)	+22 (82)	+03 (99)	−63 (132)	3.17**	2.07*
Think-Feel	+35 (127)	+41 (99)	−02 (86)	+26 (132)	−32 (122)	ns	ns
All 12 factors (multivariate test)						$F_{12,114} = 7.36$***	$F_{12,112} = 6.62$***

* $p < .05$;
** $p < .01$;
*** $p < .001$.
[a]Personal Total, World Total, and SumBound were not included in the multivariate test.
[b]Factor names are abbreviated but are listed in the original order (see Table 2, pp. 64–85).
[c]Factor scores (multiplied by 100 to remove decimals) have entire-sample means of 0.00 and standard deviations of 10. Positive factor score means indicate that the group was above the average (in the thin direction) of the 866 subjects upon which the factor analysis was based. Negative factor scores indicate that the group in question was below the average for the whole sample. A standard deviation above 100 indicates a greater-than-average degree of heterogeneity among individuals within the group.
[d]In this table the factors are entered in the thin direction—higher numbers are thinner. Thus, factor II, "Preference for Explicit Boundaries," is entered in the opposite direction as "Preference for No Explicit Boundaries" (No-Explicit). Factors VII, VIII, XI, and XII are handled similarly.

Table A-2 Statistically Significant Correlations Between Boundary Measures and K-corrected MMPI Scales in 299 Subjects[a,b,c]

Boundary Measure	MMPI Scale													
	L	F	K	HS	D	HY	PD	MF[m]	MF[f]	PA	PT	SC	MA	SI
I Primary Process	−26	+49	−45		+14		+32	+17		+43	+34	+40	+37	+20
II Dislike Explicit	−26	+25	−22		+14			+23				+21		+23
III Children	−25		−16	−12				+20	+17					
IV Fragility		+38	−33	+12	+37	+20	+38	+33		+37	+42	+31		+39
V Clairvoyance					−15	−13					−12		+24	−12
VI Openness		−13			−30		−17				−15	−16	+12	−28
VIII Intergroup		+24	−18		+15									
IX Flexibility			−14											
X Overinvolv			−12											
XI Geometric			−14						+22	+14				+20
XII Think-Feel				+12										
Personal Total	−28	+43	−46		+13		+32	+36		+46	+30	+30	+34	+15
World Total	−15			−21				+31	+21				−15	
SumBound	−31	+32	−37				+27	+40		+41	+21	+25	+30	+07

[a]Factor VII, Organized Planfulness, did not correlate with any of the MMPI scores.

[b]These correlations between boundary measures and MMPI Mf raw scores were computed separately for men and for women. The signs of the correlations for women are reversed, so that a positive correlation between a boundary score and MF for both men and for women indicates a correlation with opposite-sex identification.

[c]Factors are entered in the "thin" direction.

Table A-3 Male vs. Female Differences on the Boundary Questionnaire
(412 males, 539 females for the total scores; 399 males, 453 females for the factor scores)

	Males	*Females*	*t*	*p*	*Direction*
SumBound	263 ± 49	287 ± 50	7.6	< .0001	Males thicker
Personal Total	167 ± 40	187 ± 41	7.4	< .0001	Males thicker
World Total	96 ± 15	101 ± 15	4.7	< .0001	Males thicker
Factor 1	−0.17 ± 0.9	0.14 ± 1.0	4.6	< .0001	Males thicker
Factor 2	−0.06 ± 1.0	0.04 ± 1.0	1.5	n.s.	No signif. dif.
Factor 3	−0.13 ± 1.0	0.10 ± 1.0	3.5	< .001	Males thicker
Factor 4	−0.13 ± 1.0	0.12 ± 1.0	3.8	< .0001	Males thicker
Factor 5	−0.10 ± 0.9	0.10 ± 1.1	3.1	< .01	Males thicker
Factor 6	−0.06 ± 1.0	0.04 ± 1.0	1.6	n.s.	No signif. dif.
Factor 7	−0.08 ± 1.0	0.05 ± 1.0	1.9	n.s.	No signif. dif.
Factor 8	0.20 ± 1.0	−0.17 ± 1.0	5.4	< .0001	Females thicker
Factor 9	−0.03 ± 1.0	0.02 ± 1.0	0.8	n.s.	No signif. dif.
Factor 10	−0.03 ± 1.0	0.03 ± 1.0	0.9	n.s.	No signif. dif.
Factor 11	−0.34 ± 1.0	0.30 ± 0.9	9.7	< .0001	Males thicker
Factor 12	−0.16 ± 0.9	0.14 ± 1.0	4.3	< .0001	Males thicker

NOTE: In this table all factors are listed in the "thin" direction (positive scores are thin).

Table A-4 A Comparison of Frequent Dreamers (seven or more dreams per week) and Nondreamers

	Frequent Dreamers (N = 64)	*Nondreamers (N = 69)*	*t*	*p*
SumBound Total	314 ± 60	232 ± 40	9.2	<.0001
Personal Total	208 ± 48	142 ± 32	9.2	<.0001
World Total	106 ± 17	89 ± 17	5.6	<.0001
Sleep-Dream-Wake	23 ± 13	8 ± 7	8.6	<.0001
Unusual Experiences	34 ± 13	15 ± 9	9.5	<.0001
Thoughts, Feelings, Moods	33 ± 11	24 ± 9	5.7	<.0001
Child, Adol., Adult	13 ± 4	10 ± 4	3.3	<.01
Interpersonal	27 ± 6	23 ± 6	3.7	<.001
Sensitivity	15 ± 3	12 ± 4	4.2	<.0001
Neat, Exact, Precise	21 ± 7	18 ± 6	3.4	<.001
Edges, Lines, Clothing	41 ± 8	33 ± 8	6.3	<.0001
Opinions about Children	23 ± 5	20 ± 5	3.8	<.001
Opinions about Organizations	26 ± 6	22 ± 6	4.4	<.0001
People, Nations, Groups	38 ± 7	32 ± 8	4.5	<.0001
Beauty, Truth	19 ± 4	16 ± 4	4.1	<.0001

REFERENCES

ADAIR, H. *The relationship of Rorschach and IQ scores to Boundary Questionnaire scores.* Unpublished manuscript. Tufts University School of Medicine.

AMERICAN PSYCHIATRIC ASSOCIATION. (1980). *Diagnostic and statistical manual of mental disorders* (3rd ed.). Washington, D.C.: APA Press.

AMERICAN PSYCHIATRIC ASSOCIATION. (1987). *Diagnostic and statistical manual of mental disorders* (3rd ed., rev.). Washington, D.C.: APA Press.

ANZIEU, D. (1987). *Le moi peau.* Paris: Monod Press.

ASTON-JONES, G. and Bloom, F. E. (1981). Activity of norepinephrine-containing locus coeruleus neurons in behaving rats anticipates fluctuations in the sleep-waking cycle. *Journal of Neuroscience, 8*, 876–886.

BARON, M., Agnis, L., and Gruen, R. (1981). The schedule for schizotypal personalities (SSP): A diagnostic interview for schizotypal features. *Psychiatry Research, 4*, 213–228.

BARRETT, D. (1989, April). *The relationship of thin vs. thick boundaries to hypnotic susceptibility.* Paper presented at the meetings of the Eastern Psychological Association, Boston, Mass.

Barron, F. (1969). *Creative person and creative process.* New York: Holt, Rinehart, & Winston.

Beal, S. (1988). The boundary characteristics of artists (Doctoral dissertation, Boston University), 1989–16375. *Dissertation Abstracts International.*

Belicki, K. (1987). Recalling dreams: An examination of daily variation and individual differences. In J. Gackenbach (Ed.), *Sleep and dreams: A sourcebook* (pp. 187–206). New York: Garland Publishing.

Bergman, P., and Escalona, S. (1949). Unusual sensitivities in very young children. *The Psychoanalytic Study of the Child, 3/4,* 333–352.

Bevis, J. (1986). Connectedness vs. separateness: Understanding male/female differences in self and relationships. (Doctoral dissertation, Boston University), 47/02, 778B. *Dissertation Abstracts International.*

Blatt, S., Brenneis, C., Schmiek, J., and Glick, M. (1976). The normal developmental and psychopathological impairment of the concept of the object on the Rorschach. *Journal of Abnormal Psychology, 85,* 304–373.

Blatt, S., and Ritzler, B. (1974). Thought disorder and boundary disturbance in psychosis. *Journal of Consulting and Clinical Psychology, 42,* 370–381.

Bowers, M., Jr. (1974). *Retreat from sanity.* New York: Human Sciences Press.

Broughton, R. (1968). Sleep disorders: Disorders of arousal? *Science, 159,* 1070–1078.

Brown, D., and Fromm, E. (1987). *Hypnosis and behavioral medicine.* Hillsdale, N.J.: Lawrence Erlbaum.

Celenza, A. (1986). Empathy, ego boundaries and deficits. (Doctoral dissertation, Boston University), 47/05, 2152B. *Dissertation Abstracts International.*

Chapman, L., Chapman, J., and Raulin, M. (1978). Body image alteration in schizophrenia. *Journal of Abnormal Psychology, 87,* 399–407

Chugani, H., Phelps, M., and Mazziotta, J. (1987). Positron emission tomography study of human brain functional development. *Annals of Neurology, 22,* 487–497.

CLONINGER, C. (1986). A unified biosocial theory of personality and its role in the development of anxiety states. *Psychiatric Developments, 3*, 167–226.

CLONINGER, C. (1987). A systematic method for clinical description and clarification of personality variants. *Archives of General Psychiatry, 44*, 573–588.

COHEN, D. (1974). Toward a theory of dream recall. *Psychological Bulletin, 81,* 138–154.

COOLIDGE, C. (1933). Program for Coolidge memorial service, 1933. Coolidge Library, University of Massachusetts, Amherst, Mass.

COOPER, J., Bloom, F., and Roth, R. (1986). The biochemical basis of neuropharmacology. New York: Oxford University Press.

CORCORAN, K. (1983). Emotional separation and empathy. *Journal of Clinical Psychology, 39,* 667–671.

DAHLSTROM, W., Welsh, G., and Dahlstrom, L. (1972). *An MMPI Handbook.* Vol. 1, *Clinical interpretation* (2nd ed.). Minneapolis: University of Minnesota Press.

DEMENT, W. (1958). Occurrence of low voltage, fast electroencephalogram patterns during behavioral sleep in cats. *Electroencephalography and Clinical Neurophysiology, 10,* 291–296.

EDELMAN, G. (1987). *Neural Darwinism: The theory of neuronal group selection.* New York: Basic Books.

EDELMAN, G. (1989). *The remembered present: A biological theory of consciousness.* New York: Basic Books.

ERIKSON, E. (1950). *Childhood and society.* New York: W. W. Norton.

EXNER, J. (1986). *The Rorschach: A comprehensive system.* New York: John Wiley.

EYSENCK, H. (1967). *The biological basis of personality.* Springfield: C. C. Thomas.

EYSENCK, H. (1976). *The measurement of personality.* Baltimore: University Park Press.

FARBER, S. (1981). Identical twins raised apart: A reanalysis. New York: Basic Books

FEDERN, P. (1952). *Ego psychology and the psychoses.* New York: Basic Books.

FEINBERG, I. (1982/83). Schizophrenia: Caused by a fault in programmed synaptic elimination during adolescence? *Journal of Psychiatric Research, 17,* 319–334.

FEINBERG, I., March, J. D., Flach, K., Maloney, T., Chern, W.-J., and Travis, F. T. (1989). Late maturational decline in delta (0-3 Hz) EEG amplitude during sleep: A reflection of synaptic elimination? *Soc. Neurosci. Abs., 15* (Part 1), 244.

FEINBERG, I., Thode, H., Jr., Chugani, H., and March, J. (1990). Gamma distribution model describes maturational curves for delta wave amplitude, cortical metabolic rate and synaptic density. *Journal of Theoretical Biology, 142,* 149–161.

FISHER, S. (1986). *The development and structure of the body image.* Hillsdale, N.J.: Erlbaum.

FISHER, S., and Cleveland, S. (1968). *Body image and personality* (2nd ed.). New York: Dover.

FOULKES, D. (1966). *The psychology of sleep.* New York: Scribner.

FOULKES, D. (1985). *Dreaming: A cognitive-psychological analysis.* Hillsdale, N.J.: Erlbaum.

FREEDMAN, D. (1968). The use and abuse of LSD. *Archives of General Psychiatry, 18*, 330–347.

FREUD, A. (1946). *The ego and the mechanisms of defense.* New York: International Universities Press.

FREUD, S. (1900/1953). The interpretation of dreams. Standard Edition, vols. 4,5.

FREUD, S. (1909). Notes upon a case of obsessional neurosis. In *The standard edition of the complete psychological works of Sigmund Freud,* vol. 10 (pp. 153–249). London: Hogarth Press.

FREUD, S. (1920). Beyond the pleasure principle. In *The standard edition of the complete psychological works of Sigmund Freud,* vol. 18 (pp. 7–66). London: Hogarth Press.

FREUD, S. (1923). The ego and the id. In *The standard edition of the complete psychological works of Sigmund Freud,* vol. 19 (pp. 3–66). London: Hogarth Press.

FREUD, S. (1924). A note upon the "mystic writing pad." In *The standard edition of the complete psychological works of Sigmund Freud,* vol. 19 (pp. 237–232). London: Hogarth Press.

FREUD, S. (1925). Inhibitions, symptoms, and anxiety. In *The standard edition of the complete psychological works of Sigmund Freud,* vol. 20 (pp. 77–174). London: Hogarth Press.

FREUD, S. (1898/1954). *The origins of psychoanalysis.* New York: Basic Books.

GALVIN, F. (1990). The boundary characteristics of lucid dreamers. *Psychiatric Journal of the University of Ottawa, 15,* 73–78.

GARDNER, R., Holzman, P., Klein, G., Linton, H., and Spence, D. (1959). Cognitive control: A study of individual consistencies in cognitive behavior. *Psychological Issues,* Monograph 4. New York: International Universities Press.

GARG, M., and Hartmann, E. (To be published). *The neuropsychology of personality: People with "thick" or "thin" boundaries.*

GILLIGAN, C. (1982). *In a different voice.* Cambridge: Harvard University Press.

GOODENOUGH, D. (1974). Dream recall: History and current states of the field. In Arkin, A., Antrobus, J., and Ellman, S., eds. *The mind in sleep.* Hillsdale, N.J.: Lawrence Erlbaum.

GRAHAM, J. (1977). *The MMPI: A practical guide.* New York: Oxford University Press.

GUILFORD, J., Frick, J., Christensen, P., and Merrifield, P. (1957). A factor-analytic study of flexibility in thinking. *University of Southern California Laboratory Reports,* no. 18.

HALL, C., and Lindzey, G. (1978). *Theories of personality.* New York: Wiley.

HARRISON, R., Hartmann, E., and Bevis, J. (to be published). *The Hartmann boundary questionnaire: A measure of thin and thick boundaries.*

HARTMANN, E. (1973). *The functions of sleep.* New Haven: Yale University Press.

HARTMANN, E. (1976). The dream as the royal road to the biology of the mental apparatus. *International Journal of Psychoanalysis, 57,* 331–334.

HARTMANN, E. (1978). *The sleeping pill.* New Haven: Yale University Press.

HARTMANN, E. (1982). From the biology of dreaming to the biology of the mind. *The Psychoanalytic Study of the Child, 37,* 303–335.

HARTMANN, E. (1984). *The Nightmare.* New York: Basic Books.

Hartmann, E., Baekeland, F., and Zwilling, G. (1972). Psychological differences between long and short sleepers. *Archives of General Psychiatry, 26,* 463–468.

Hartmann, E., Baekeland, F., Zwilling, G., and Hoy, P. (1971). Sleep need: How much sleep and what kind? *American Journal of Psychiatry, 127,* 1001–1008.

Hartmann, E., and Brewer, V. (1976). When is more or less sleep required: A study of variable sleepers. *Comprehensive Psychiatry, 17,* 275–284.

Hartmann, E., Elkin, R., and Garg, M. (In press). The dreams of people with thick or thin boundaries. *Dreaming.*

Hartmann, E., Mehta, N., Forgione, A., Brune, P., and LaBrie, R. (1987a). Bruxism: Effects of alcohol. *Sleep Research, 16,* 351.

Hartmann, E., Mehta, N., Forgione, A., Brune, P., and LaBrie, R. (1987b). Bruxism: Personality traits and other characteristics. *Sleep Research, 16,* 350.

Hartmann, E., Milofsky, E., Vaillant, G., Oldfield, M., Falke, R., and Ducey, C. (1984). Vulnerability to schizophrenia: Prediction of adult schizophrenia using childhood information. *Archives of General Psychiatry, 41*, 1050–1056.

Hartmann, E., Russ, D., van der Kolk, B., Falke, R., and Oldfield, M. (1981). A preliminary study of the personality of the nightmare sufferer: Relationship to schizophrenia and creativity? *The American Journal of Psychiatry, 138,* 794–797.

Hartmann, E., Russ, D., Oldfield, M., Sivan, I., and Cooper, S. (1987). Who has nightmares? The personality of the lifelong nightmare sufferer. *Archives of General Psychiatry, 44,* 49–56.

Hartmann, E., Sivan, I., Cooper, S., and Treger, F. (1984). The personality of lifelong nightmare sufferers: Projective test results. *Sleep Research, 13,* 118.

Herman, J., Perry, J., van der Kolk, B. (1989). Childhood trauma in borderline personality disorder. *American Journal of Psychiatry, 146,* 490–495.

Hippocrates. The Sacred Disease, XVII. In G. Lloyd, ed. (1978). *Hippocratic Writings.* J. Chadwick and W. Mann, trans. New York: Penguin.

Hobson, J. A., McCarley, R. W., and Nelson, J. P. (1983). Location and spike-train characteristics of cells in anterodorsal pons having selective decreases in firing rat during desynchronized sleep. *Journal of Neurophysiology, 50*, 770–783.

Holzman, P., Proctor, L., Levy, D., Yasillo, N., Meltzer, H., and Hurt, S. (1974). Eye-tracking dysfunctions in schizophrenic patients and their relatives. *Archives of General Psychiatry, 31,* 143–151.

Huttenlocher, P. (1979). Synaptic density in human frontal cortex—Developmental changes and effects of aging. *Brain Research, 163,* 195–205.

James, W. (1907). *Pragmatism: A new name for some old ways of thinking.* New York: Longmans Green. Reprinted. New York: Washington Square Press, 1983.

Jernigan, T., and Tallal, P. (1990). Late changes in brain morphology observable with MRI. *Developmental Medicine and Child Neurology, 32,* 379–385.

Johnson, D., and Quinlan, D. (1980). Fluid and rigid boundaries of paranoid and nonparanoid schizophrenics on a role-playing task. *Journal of Personality Assessment, 44,* 523–531.

Jouvet, M. (1962). Recherches sur les structures nerveuses et les mécanismes responsables des différentes phases du sommeil physiologique. *Arch. Ital. Biol., 100,* 125–206.

Jung, C. (1921). Psychological types. *Collected works of C. G. Jung.* Princeton: Bollingen.

Kandel, E. (1984). Steps toward a molecular basis for learning: Explorations into the nature of memory. In J. Isselbacher (Ed.), *Medicine, science and society.* New York: Wiley.

Kantor, D., and Lehr, W. (1975). *Inside the family.* San Francisco: Jossey-Bass.

Karacan, I., Williams, R., and Moore, C. (Eds.). (1988). *Sleep disorders: Diagnoses and treatment.* New York: Wiley.

Kety, S., Rosenthal, D., Wender, P., Schulsinger, F., and Jacobson, B. (1975). Mental illness in the biological and adoptive families of adopted individuals who have become schizophrenic. In R. F. Dieve, H. Brill, and D. Rosenthal (Eds.), *Genetic research in psychiatry.* Baltimore: Johns Hopkins University Press.

KIPLING, R. (1953). If. In B. Stevenson (Ed.). *The home book of verse.* New York: Holt, Rinehart & Winston.

KRIS, E. (1952). *Psychoanalytic explorations in art.* New York: International Universities Press.

KRYGER, M., Roth, T., and Dement, W. (Eds.). (1989). *Principles and practice of sleep medicine.* Philadelphia: W.B. Saunders.

KUNZENDORF, R., and Sheikh, A. (1990). Imaging, image-monitoring, and health. In R. Kunzendorf and A. Sheikh (Eds.), *The psychophysiology of mental imagery.* Amityville, N.Y.: Baywood.

LANDIS, B. (1970). Ego boundaries. *Psychological Issues, 6*(4), Monograph #24. New York: International Universities Press.

LEVIN, R. (1986). Ego boundary impairment and thought disorder in frequent nightmare sufferers: Evidence for a proposed pathognomonic relationship to schizophrenia. (Doctoral dissertation, University of Buffalo).

LEVIN, R., and Galin, J. (1991). Nightmares, boundaries, and creativity. *Dreaming, 1*, 63–74.

LEVIN, R., and Raulin, M. (In press). Preliminary evidence for the proposed relationship between frequent nightmares and schizotypal symptomatology. *Journal of Personality Disorders.*

LEWIN, K. (1935). *A dynamic theory of personality.* New York: McGraw-Hill.

LEWIN, K. (1936). *Principles of topological psychology.* New York: McGraw-Hill.

MEDNICK, S. (1962). The associative basis of the creative process. *Psychological Review, 69,* 220–232.

MEISSNER, W. (1985). Theories of personality and psychopathology: Classical psychoanalysis. In H. Kaplan and B. Sadock (Eds.), *Comprehensive textbook of psychiatry/IV* (4th ed.). Baltimore: Williams & Wilkins.

METZ, J., Pivik, R., and Rechtschaffer, A. (1975). Phasic facial and extraocular muscle activity during sleep in cats and humans. *Sleep Research, 4*, 35.

MILLER, J. (1986). *Toward a new psychology of women* (2nd ed.). Boston: Beacon Press.

MODELL, A. (1975). A narcissistic defence against affects and the illusion of self-sufficiency. *International Journal of Psychoanalysis, 56,* 275–282.

Molin, C., and Levi, L. (1966). A psycho-odontologic investigation of patients with bruxism. *Acta Odontologica Scandinavica, 24*, 373–391.

Myers, I. (1962). *The Myers-Briggs Type Indicator.* Palo Alto: Consulting Psychologists Press.

Norman, W. (1963). Toward an adequate taxonomy of personality attributes: Replicated factor structure in peer nomination personality ratings. *Journal of Abnormal and Social Psychology, 66,* 574–583.

Noshpitz, J., ed. (1970). *Basic handbook of child psychiatry.* Volume I: Development. New York: Basic Books.

Rapaport, D. (1960). *The structure of psychoanalytic theory: A systematizing attempt.* New York: International Universities Press.

Reich, W. (1933). *Charakter analyse.* Vienna: Sexpol Verlag.

Shapiro, D. (1965). *Neurotic styles.* New York: Basic Books.

Sheikh, A., and Kunzendorf, R. (1984). Imagery, physiology, and psychosomatic illness. *International Review of Mental Imagery, 1,* 95–138.

Shields, J. (1962). Monozygotic twins brought up apart and brought up together. London: Oxford University Press.

Siegel, J., and Rogawski, M. (1988). A function for REM sleep: Regulation of noradrenergic receptor sensitivity. *Brain Research Reviews, 13,* 213–233.

Siever, L., Coursey, R., Alterman, I., Buchsbaum, M., and Murphy, D. (1984). Impaired smooth pursuit eye movement: Vulnerability marker for schizotypal personality disorder in a normal volunteer population. *American Journal of Psychiatry, 141,* 1560–1566.

Siever, L., Coursey, R., Alterman, I., Zahn, T., Brody, L., Bernad, P., Buchsbaum, M., Lake, C., and Murphy, D. (1989). Clinical, psychophysiological, and neurological characteristics of volunteers with impaired smooth pursuit eye movements. *Biological Psychiatry, 26,* 35–51.

Sivan, I. (1983). *Anxiety and ego functions of nightmare dreamers.* Unpublished Masters thesis, Haifa University.

Tellegen, A., and Atkinson, G. (1974). Openness to absorbing and self-altering experiences ("absorption"): A trait related to hypnotic susceptibility. *Journal of Abnormal Psychology, 83,* 268–277.

van der Kolk, B., Blitz, R., Burr, W., Sherry, S., and Hartmann, E. (1984). Nightmares and trauma: A comparison of nightmares after combat with lifelong nightmares in veterans. *American Journal of Psychiatry, 141,* 187–190.

Watson, R. (1985, July). Phasic integrated potentials and ego boundary deficit. Paper presented to a joint meeting of the Sleep Research Society and the Association of Sleep Disorders Centers, Seattle, Washington.

Webb, W. (1979). Psychological reports, *44,* 259–264.

Webb, W., and Agnew, H., Jr. (1970). Sleep stage characteristics of long and short sleepers. *Science, 168,* 146–147.

Webb, W. and Friel, J. (1970). Characteristics of "natural" long and short sleepers: A preliminary report. *Psychol. Reports, 27*, 63–66.

Weider, A., Wolff, H., Brodman, K., Mittelmann, B., and Wechsler, D. (1944). *The Cornell index.* New York: The Psychological Corporation.

Weiner, H. (1977). *Psychobiology and human disease.* New York: Elsevier.

Winget, C., and Kramer, M. (1979). *Dimensions of dreams.* Gainesville: University Presses of Florida.

Wood, J., and Bootzin, R. (1990). The prevalence of nightmares and their independence from anxiety. *Journal of Abnormal Psychology, 99,* 64–68.

Yeats, W. (1951). A prayer for old age. In *The collected poems of W.B. Yeats.* New York: Macmillan.

Zetzel, E. (1970). *The capacity for emotional growth.* New York: International Universities Press.

Zuckerman, M., Buchsbaum, M., and Murphy, D. (1980). Sensation-seeking and its biological correlates. *Psychological Bulletin, 88,* 187–214.

INDEX

2.5

145 | 367

290

770

725